# Advertising God

Thanks for supporting the
Advertising God ministry.
I hope you find the
Scriptures and principles
within to be beneficial to
you as you share your
faith story with those
you come into contact with.
Remember Galatians 1:10 in
all you say and do.

Rick D.

# Advertising God

✦

## Shamelessly Promote and Share Your Faith with Anyone, Anytime, Anyplace

*Rick Sizemore*

iUniverse, Inc.
New York Lincoln Shanghai

# Advertising God
## Shamelessly Promote and Share Your Faith with Anyone, Anytime, Anyplace

iUniverse books may be ordered through booksellers or by contacting:

iUniverse
2021 Pine Lake Road, Suite 100
Lincoln, NE 68512
www.iuniverse.com
1-800-Authors (1-800-288-4677)

ISBN-13: 978-0-595-40694-4 (pbk)
ISBN-13: 978-0-595-85058-7 (ebk)
ISBN-10: 0-595-40694-7 (pbk)
ISBN-10: 0-595-85058-8 (ebk)

Printed in the United States of America

For my wife Lisa, my mother and my late grandmother, a trio of the most inspiring women I've ever known. And to Almighty God of course, for without His love, guidance, infinite creativity and blessing, this book would have remained just wishful thinking.

# Contents

# Introduction

*"You've got cancer."* It was August 1991 and those three words changed the course of my life. Earlier that afternoon, my ophthalmologist discovered a tumor rudely lodged in my left eye. Only about the size of the head of a thumbtack, it was too large to kill with radiation and removing the tumor wasn't possible. The doctor informed me that the only other treatment protocol was enucleation, or complete removal of the eye. I was 29 years old, a newlywed and frightened beyond belief.

That night, following lots of tearful hugging with my wife, I did something I hadn't done in years—I prayed. Although I was raised in a Baptist church and had accepted Christ when I was twelve, I had fallen away from the church in my college years and in doing so had stepped away from God. But during those frightening hours after my initial diagnosis, I knew I needed to come back to God and reach out for Him. So I prayed for a miracle, for a cancer-free body and for restoration of my health. I pleaded with God to summon up all His healing power and make that cancer disappear. Although I lost my eye, God did indeed heal me because removal of my eye meant the cancer was gone from my body and that my long-term prognosis was excellent. As of 2006, I've been cancer-free for 15 years. Praise God!

I know it sounds strange, but my bout with cancer wasn't such a bad thing because it dramatically altered my spiritual course and ended up making me a better all-around person. Cancer caused me to take an introspective look at myself and reflect on my reason for being. I wondered why was I cured when so many other cancer patients were not, and deep down, I felt like there was some life purpose God had in mind for me to fulfill. I didn't have survivor's guilt. I had sinner's remorse and a real spiritual need to re-connect with God. Cancer was a wake-up call for me to re-examine my life, set new priorities and seek out God's plan and act on it as quickly as possible. I didn't know it at the time, but that period of self-reflection was the genesis for this book.

Following my recuperation, I returned to church with more passion, more excitement and with a deeper desire to know and experience God so I could discover and faithfully execute the plan God was mapping out for me. I participated in a nine-month Bible study. I went to Sunday school and began regularly teaching the class. I shared my cancer story and my testimony. Yet all this spiritual rebirth and newfound religious intensity didn't always make it easier for me to tell others about God, commit to repentance or be the one who readily jumped at the chance to volunteer for service or mission work within the church.

Truthfully, I had an easier time talking about good books, restaurants, sports and the like than I did about God and all His blessings. And it frustrated me, especially when I considered all God had done for me. I could eagerly and enthusiastically "advertise" books and restaurants with glowing compliments and superlatives, but when it came time to let others see or hear Jesus Christ living in and working through me, more often than not I would clam up, becoming guarded and hesitant, fearful of what others might say or think.

Maybe some of this sounds familiar to you because the same hesitancy to speak up for God or act positively on His behalf happens in your life, too. As a Christian, you love God and have accepted Christ as your savior, but maybe you're not totally sure you're the kind of staunch, steadfast believer God can count on minute by minute, hour by hour, day by day. You wonder what you can do to improve your resolve, what you can do to strengthen your faith, what you can do to show others you are a dedicated follower of Jesus Christ. And that's where this book comes in.

The purpose of *Advertising God* is to equip Christians of all ages and denominations struggling to live out their faith with the courage and confidence needed to freely and faithfully "advertise" or promote God in any and all situations through their words, actions and deeds. It's more than sharing your faith with non-believers or inviting people to church. Advertising God encompasses all the things you say and do every day that show others the way to the cross and to a more faithful and service-oriented lifestyle. Christians and non-Christians alike see Christ living in and working through you and hopefully want to experience that same kind of love and passion in their own life. Don't underestimate your words and actions. The power of advertising God generates lots of sway on others around you and can be downright contagious.

Intended to be a primer on how to overcome the obstacles that inhibit your ability to promote God, this book also offers sound Biblical-based solutions you can use to help conquer your fears and embrace your spiritual gifts so you can do whatever it is you feel God is leading you to do. Along with practical advice, the book also weaves in time-tested strategies learned and practiced in my sixteen plus years in the advertising and marketing business that I feel Christian believers can use to help persuade others to "buy" into Christ's salvation and teachings.

Most chapters contain an *Advertising God in Real Life* section, which is a short fictional anecdote showcasing how everyday people just like you find positive and productive ways to share their faith at work and in the community, use their spiritual gifts and talents, or get more involved in the church and in God's work. My hope is that the examples of their courage, faithfulness and fortitude will inspire you to boldly stand up for God in similar situations.

One of the takeaway goals of this book is that its message will encourage you not just to act, but also to think about your Christian role and influence as well. That's why Chapters 1-10 conclude with an Up For Discussion section that has several thought-provoking questions individual readers can ponder for themselves or address and discuss corporately in a small group or Sunday school class setting. Either way, the questions are meant to facilitate introspection and galvanize conversation. If you're in a group, encourage members to answer freely without fear of reprisal and judgment. There are no right and wrong answers and your perspective may or may not agree with others.

I was once in a Sunday school class where one guy in particular always seemed to have very interesting opinions on discussion topics. Although his responses were honest and forthright, they were usually quite different from others offered up by the class. Sometimes his take was so unique, no one could quite figure out where he was coming from. But other times his answers and arguments, along with the questions he raised, sparked good conversation and debate. I didn't always agree with him, but many mornings I came away with a better understanding of Scripture because of his position.

As you read and ponder the principles in this book, I encourage you think about where you are in your own spiritual life, where you want to be, and what you can do to serve God on a daily basis. Do you love God and have such passion for Him that people quickly identify you as a Christian, or are they surprised to find out you're a Christian because your actions and your lifestyle aren't in harmony with the teachings of Christ? Are you the once-a-week Christian who shows up at church on Sunday, then "disguises" your Christian self during the week so as not be labeled, mocked or frowned upon by friends and coworkers, or are you the kind of Christian who lives by the credo in Galatians 1:10? Are you a Christian who puts God first at all costs, or one who values your career, your money, your reputation and your leisure activities more than your relationship with God?

One of the things that makes *Advertising God* so unique is that I'm not a minister, counselor or church leader. I'm simply a normal everyday Christian guy who loves God, yet wrestles with these very same issues myself. I wrote this book as much for me as for you. Because I've been there and *not* said this and *not* done that I know what it's like and how it feels to stand down instead of standing up willingly and fearlessly for God with unbridled passion, confidence and authority. Like you, I have real human weaknesses, fears and insecurities, and go through times when I shuffle back and forth between periods of faithfulness and faithful-less.

That's why the tone of this book is definitely not preachy, judgmental or academic in nature. It's empathetic and supportive. By reading and applying the principles discussed here, you will grow more confident and comfortable discussing matters of Jesus Christ in and out of the safety of your comfort zone. You'll learn to please God instead of other people. You will be challenged to seek out your spiritual gift(s) and use those gifts to benefit and glorify God's kingdom. And, you will be emboldened to grow in your faith by identifying and overcoming obstacles and excuses that hinder your desire and ability to advertise God.

Whether you're struggling to share your beliefs with others, seeking to strengthen your relationship with Christ, or you're a regular church attendee who needs encouragement and motivation to put your faith into action, a new Christian wanting practical advice, or a mature Christian looking for ways to stay fresh as you share Christ's message, you'll find something useful here. Remember, advertising God doesn't have to be some elaborate, well thought out plan or a grand production. It's usually the simple things you say and do every single day that convey a faithful and obedient Christian attitude to others.

When you shamelessly promote and share your faith with anyone, anytime and anyplace, think of all the good you do, the love you share, and the meaningful difference you make in someone's physical and spiritual life. Advertising God isn't about waffling back and forth between serving and not serving God, making excuses as to why God can't use you, or passing the buck and hoping someone else will do it. Advertising God is an outward and visible sign of your devotion to Jesus Christ and it starts squarely with you.

# 1

# *What is Advertising God?*

○ ○ ○ ○ ○ ○ ○ ○ ○ ○ ○ ○ ○ ○ ○ ○ ○ ○ ○ ○ ○ ○ ○ ○ ○ ○ ○ ○ ○ ○

"And whatever you do, whether in word or deed, do it all in the name of the Lord Jesus, giving thanks to God the Father through Him."

*—{ Colossians 3:17 }*

Being one third Italian on her mother's side, Marcy is a woman who knows and loves good, authentic Tuscan food. So when the new Italian restaurant Zanipolo's opened down the street from her home, Marcy tossed her husband Frank the car keys and off they went.

Expecting the usual pedestrian fare and teenage servers that were hallmarks of all the so-called Italian restaurants and bistros that had come and gone in the area before, Marcy was pleasantly surprised to discover this restaurant appeared to be the real deal. Everything from the beef carpaccio to the chicken marsala to the cannolis was genuine Italian through and through, and the wait staff was personable, attentive and knowledgeable about the food and its preparation. Even chef Zanipolo himself was born and raised in Trieste.

The food and service were so good, Marcy had a standing reservation twice a week to eat at Zanipolo's. When she wasn't there, she raved about chef Z and his creative cuisine to her friends and friends of friends, her hairdresser, her exercise class and her coworkers. If the topic of food ever came up, everyone knew Marcy would jump in and plug her favorite Italian restaurant with great enthusiasm. It wasn't long before Marcy's friends began calling her Mozzarella Marcy because she bragged on Zanipolo's so much.

Isn't that the way it is with you, too? If you found a fabulous product that exceeded your expectations, dined on exceptionally fine food, or received superior customer service, wouldn't you tell people you know about your experience?

1

Wouldn't you enthusiastically recommend that product, restaurant or store on a regular basis? As consumers who find comfort and security in the sanctuary of shared experience, our desire is to tell others about our positive encounters in the marketplace hoping they will have as good as an experience, if not a better one, than we had.

It's the same unabashed enthusiasm and conviction you should have as you serve, worship and praise our Holy God. That exuberant, almost euphoric feeling that comes from knowing you've been saved and redeemed by the blood and grace of Jesus Christ. That joy and peace you gain by accepting Christ and reserving a place in His eternal kingdom. There ought to be a part of you that can't wait to share your faith and testimony with others so they don't miss out on experiencing the joy and peace that comes from having a personal relationship with Jesus Christ.

I call this kind of impassioned joy advertising God. Advertising God simply means letting others know you are a dedicated, faithful and loving Christian servant through your words, actions and deeds. It means instead of privatizing your beliefs, you go public with them. Instead of hiding behind your faith, you courageously live it out for all to see. Instead of feeling ashamed at being labeled a Christian, you rejoice in it.

Maybe this already sounds a lot like you. Maybe you're the kind of person who actively and passionately talks up God or does good works for Him in any situation without fear, hesitation or concerns about your reputation around the office or neighborhood. That's great! You're advertising God with an obedient heart and faithfully living out Christ's command in the Great Commission.

But many other Christians wonder why is it easier to talk about good mechanics, honest contractors and delicious cheeseburgers than it is about God. Why it's easier to spread the news about a great sale at the mall than it is to spread the good news of Jesus Christ? Why it's easier to invite friends to a favorite restaurant than it is to invite them to church? Why it's easier to sit down than stand up for our Christian beliefs? Why it's easier for us to promote secular self-help books than it is the Bible (which, ironically, is the ultimate self-help book!)?

There's no easy answer, of course. There's just something about verbally sharing your faith or engaging in acts that are overtly Christian that sometimes makes you feel uncomfortable. As a believer who adamantly professes to love and follow Christ, you know it shouldn't be this way. And you're right. When it comes to talking up all the wonderful benefits and features of God the Father Almighty and Jesus Christ, too many times we let opportunity after opportunity slip by without saying a single word to praise Jesus Christ or without lifting a finger to participate in God's work, ministries or outreach programs.

And that's not how God wants His people to be. If living the Christian life was played out like a sporting event, this kind of passive and indifferent behavior would be tantamount to blowing a save, shanking a punt, clanging a dunk off the back iron, or muffing a game-winning touchdown pass. Unlike big-time sports however, thousands of watchful eyes probably aren't on you when you drop the ball, but God's eyes are. He's your biggest fan and the one you disappoint most when you fail to publicize all His winning attributes.

After listening to other Christians and hearing about their struggles and insecurities over sharing and expressing their faith, God enlightened me with one of those classic "a-ha" moments. I realized my inadequacies as a "salesperson" for God was not unique. Nor was the problem mine and mine alone to battle. Just like me, there are plenty of fearful and apprehensive Christians out there who consistently struggle with the very same issues when it comes to sharing and living true to their faith. Maybe you are one of them. The mere fact you're reading this book means you probably are. But that doesn't make you a bad person or a bad believer. None of us is perfect. We Christians are all in this advertising God thing together, and we want to find productive and tangible ways to shed our fears and insecurities and promote God with the excitement and passion we know He requires and deserves.

God laid the challenge of addressing these very issues on my heart, and being employed in the advertising business, I began to question if some of the same principles of secular advertising could be applied to the faith lives of Christians to help us become more passionate, confident and effective witnesses, or advertisers, for Christ. As a copywriter, I'm paid by my clients to promote a wide array of products without ever being at a loss for words. Why should talking up God be any different, I wondered. He is, after all, the greatest "product" known to humankind!

As God worked within me, the idea of writing this book took root. Much like Elijah's experience in the Old Testament, God's plan for me wasn't exposed in the rumbling staccato of a powerful thunderstorm, but in a gentle, persistent whisper. Maybe you know the kind of whisper I'm talking about. Soft enough to easily ignore or discount, but dogged enough that you come to know it's what God wants you to do. Perhaps like me, you were uncertain how exactly to proceed, unsure if that something dogging you really is God's plan for you, and if it is, you struggle to get past feeling so very unworthy to even attempt such a task. Yet consider and choose you God does in spite of all your shortcomings. I wasn't sure exactly what to write or even where to begin, but I recalled Samuel's response as God was summoning him, "Here I am, Lord, your servant is listening."

Has God been whispering to you, challenging you to pursue a mission or worship opportunity, reach out to someone in need, volunteer to teach Sunday school, join a Bible study, or get more involved in the church? Be like Samuel. Let God know you hear what He is saying and that you're ready, willing and able to shift your faith into high gear and drive others to a happier, more fulfilled life in Jesus Christ.

## Little Things Make a Big Difference

Advertising God isn't just talking the talk. It's also walking the walk. It is the little things you do every day that show others you are a dedicated follower of Christ. It doesn't have to be some elaborate message or presentation. It can be as simple as wearing a cross or religious-themed jewelry, inviting someone to church, saying the blessing before a meal, sharing your spiritual values with a friend or coworker, reading your Bible on a commuter train or airplane, leading a prayer, listening to Christian music at home or in your car, or performing a random act of kindness in Christ's name. The point is, advertising God is not always overt. More often than not, advertising God is usually something simple, unplanned and unrehearsed.

Whether in one-on-one conversation, heading up a Bible study group, or counseling a friend, advertising God is something every Christian is called—and expected—to do. Instead of always asking God to do for you, perhaps it's time you started asking what you can do for God by taking advantage of the personality characteristics and gifts you've been blessed with. Watch those who fervently and successfully advertise God and you'll see they possess such traits as empathy, imagination, objectivity, persistence, creativity, patience and humility. They don't shy away from opportunities to share their love for God and neither should you.

When you consider all the things Jesus has done for you, you should be so fired up for Christ you can hardly contain your joy. You should always be ready to tell anyone, anytime and anywhere what an amazing God you love and worship, and how He has impacted your life in countless and immeasurable ways. This kind of inner happiness should be like a message you can't wait to deliver, a zealous exuberance you simply cannot contain. You should want to get out there and start telling others just how awesome God really is. Take inspiration from the ever-popular Energizer Bunny and just keep witnessing and witnessing and witnessing. Even in the face of adversity, the bunny always keeps going and going and so should you. But it's the getting going that is part of the problem many Christians face.

## We Must Become the Change We Wish to See

Most of us have a strong desire to do God's work and help make the world a better place, so no Christ-centered believer intentionally sets out to deny or disobey God. Certainly the headstrong disciple Peter didn't. But like so many of us in our daily experiences, Peter found himself in a chaotic and confusing situation where he could either boldly declare his faith or fearfully retreat into silence. It's the same with many Christians today. We proudly proclaim we love the Lord with all our heart at church, when we're in prayer or socializing with like-minded individuals, but when it comes time to put our faith into action or seek praise opportunities outside of our comfort zone, many of these same Christians find it's much easier and much safer to avoid the "dangers" of being known as a follower of Christ. They simply pass up one chance after another to advertise God rather than risk the possibility of contempt, embarrassment or alienation from friends and peers.

So how do you reinvent yourself and change from one who avoids advertising God to one who sincerely enjoys and actively seeks out opportunities to shamelessly promote God? Mahatma Gandhi wrote, "You must be the change you wish to see in the world."[1] To help you achieve true change, you have to unburden yourself from all the obstacles, inhibitions and bad habits that prevent you becoming an impassioned advertiser of God. Stop letting your action, or inaction as it were, be governed by fear and tentativeness and start being receptive to God's love and guidance in your life. And instead of trusting God only up to a certain point, place your confidence wholly and completely in God and let Him lead you where He wants you to go. While it's true God never promises the life of a Christian believer will be a bed of roses, He does pledge to strengthen and empower you through the Holy Spirit when you get pricked by all those thorns along the way. So cast aside your doubts and insecurities, and become more responsive to letting God work through you and your abilities to accomplish great and mighty things. You'll be amazed at all you and God can do!

*Advertising God in Real Life:*

*The men's group at Thomas' church has a weekend retreat coming up. The retreat's theme is Breaking the Power of Lust and Addiction. Thomas, himself a recovering alcoholic, has been asked to be one of the Saturday morning speakers, and he is excited about sharing his testimony with a large group. For some time, he has been praying for God to help him turn his weakness into a powerful tool he can use to help others struggling with similar problems.*

*A few weeks before the retreat, Thomas gets an e-mail from his boss informing Thomas that he will be needed that very same Saturday morning to deliver an important presentation. Thomas calls his boss back, explains his conflict and requests the presentation be rescheduled. His boss says no, the meeting must proceed as planned. Could another manager make the presentation, Thomas asks. Again, his boss answers no. Making these kinds of presentations was one of Thomas' strengths, after all.*

*Thomas hangs up confused and dejected. On the one hand, he doesn't want to miss the opportunity God has given him to share his faith. On the other, Thomas certainly doesn't want to jeopardize his career. After much hand wringing, Thomas feels there is only one choice he can make. He starts to call the retreat leader and cancel his speaking engagement, but has the nagging feeling that this is very much a watershed moment in his faith life. He replaces the phone and immediately begins to pray. Later that night Thomas feels God strongly giving him the answer to his dilemma.*

*Though concerned about his job security, Thomas calls his boss first thing the next morning to inform him that he must honor his original commitment to speak at the retreat. The company will simply have to get someone else to make the presentation or reschedule it. The boss is frustrated, but agrees to see what he can do. Thomas nearly begins to acquiesce, but decides to abide by his decision regardless of the consequences.*

*Thomas advertises God by putting Christ first even in the face of potential job loss or reprimand.*

In Philippians 4:9, Paul encourages the believers in Philippi by writing "Whatever you have learned or received or heard from me, or seen in me—put it into practice." These very words could have come as a directive from Christ himself during His ministry time on earth. Effectively advertising God requires you to do more than just read the Bible, say a prayer every so often or listen to a sermon once a week. It calls you to put your faith into action whatever the circumstances may be. If you find that you're hesitant, consider that God may have put you in this very position on this very day for this very reason—to share your witness, to offer a loving Christian hand, to make it known you are a dedicated follower of Jesus Christ. He puts you in the right place at the right time. All you have to do is trust God to give you the courage and the words. Don't risk being like Peter and deny your faith, even if you're not sure what the reaction or outcome will be.

## Being a Christian Isn't a Part-Time Job

Advertising God touts the benefits of the risen Lord and eternal life, and informs others of who God is and how He conducts business. You can't sit back and hope someone else does the job. You have to get involved. It's up to Christian believers like you and I to promote God by putting our faith into action in the best ways we know how and by taking full advantage of our spiritual gifts. On God's team, there are no second-stringers. It's time for Christians to get up off the bench and get actively involved in the game, especially if you're one who has been riding the pines for way too long. To borrow another analogy, it's time to come out of the darkness so you can be seen living and testifying in the light. Now, more than ever, Christian action and voices need to be seen and heard. You have to be loud and proud. It is your time to stand up and like Samuel declare, "Here I am, Lord."

You can't turn your Christianity on and off or just walk and talk like a Christian when you feel like it. When we accept Christ as our personal Lord and Savior and pledge to put Him first, we are called into active duty, working to complete the ongoing task of promoting God to people of all faiths and denominations, not just the select few we deem worthy or the ones we associate with inside our community circle.

In this era of political correctness and the "if-it-feels-good-do-it" mentality, perhaps you too have expressed the same lament as the prophet Isaiah when he cries out in 42:14, "For a long time I have kept silent, I have been quiet and held myself back." Notice how Isaiah's words resonate with regret and missed opportunity. Maybe you've felt the same sting after missing out on a golden chance to advertise God. Don't think of advertising God as an intrusive and burdensome part of the Christian lifestyle. Consider it a joyful honor and privilege to advertise God! After all, He's chosen you to be His messenger here, there and everywhere your faith journey takes you.

## Learn to Please God, Not People

I can't tell you how many times I've had a simple witnessing opportunity handed right to me by God, and I fearfully let the moment pass without so much as saying a word or making a move to get involved. I was afraid of what that person or group might think of me, what they might say about me, and of repercussions that may follow. In hindsight, most of those fears were greatly exaggerated and unfounded. Nevertheless, at the time the fears had a pronounced affect on my ability to be the kind of courageous Christian witness God could count on every single day.

Maybe you can relate to these feelings. The apostle Paul certainly could. In Galatians 1:10, he addresses this very real human condition when he writes, "Am I now trying to win the approval of men or of God? If I were still trying to please men, I would not be a servant of Christ." This scripture verse captures the very essence of this book. When trying to please people rather than obey God, many of us find ourselves fearfully retreating instead of faithfully and confidently stepping forward with that "here I am" attitude God desires of all who sincerely and completely dedicate their lives to Jesus Christ. Far too often we're more concerned about what other people think about us than what God thinks about us. Today, when speech and actions are restrained under the guise of political correctness, some of us dare not say or do anything that could possibly offend certain groups or individuals. I assure you, however, that watering down God's message in order to prevent hurting someone's feelings or to protect your reputation is extremely offensive to our Lord and Savior. And ultimately, it is His opinion of you that really matters, not what other humans think. As a disciple of Christ, you are not called to tell people only what they *want* to hear, but to tell them all the things God says they *need* to hear.

If the description above sounds like you, you're probably wondering what you can do differently in your approach to creating a more Christ-focused lifestyle and attitude. First of all, be extremely proud of your spiritual beliefs and the holy God you worship and serve. Give praise and thanks to Him every chance you get, not just when it's convenient and "safe" for you. Don't worry about whether it's the right or wrong time or who is around to see and hear you. Who cares what other people think? You're here to please Christ, not other people.

You cannot be an effective witness for Christ while simultaneously trying to placate others through your words and actions. You must abide by your commitment to Christ and diligently go about the business of advertising God regardless of what others say or think about what you are doing. When Christians act as if people hold the key to our salvation, they shackle themselves to their own wants and desires and lose their spiritual focus by putting those same wants and needs before God.

Ideally, as you grow in your relationship with Jesus Christ, the louder your praises should become and the more you should want to hype His amazing love, forgiveness, guidance and salvation grace with all those around you. When people see and hear you praising God and His perpetual fountain of grace, they too want to experience the same kind of unrestrained joy and servitude as you. They look at you and wonder what you have that they don't. Your advertising influence can help foster a real desire in others to reap the benefits of everything God promises to those who accept Him.

Jesus Christ willingly endured a painful, humiliating death to save you and I from eternal separation from God. Jesus was beaten, tortured, ridiculed, spat upon and humiliated. Jesus could have simply walked away from it all, but He faithfully fulfilled God's divine purpose up until His very last breath. Considering all that Christ did and does for us still, the very least we can do is unceasingly honor, serve and praise Him for as long as we inhabit this earth.

## You Don't Have to be in Sales to be a Salesperson for God

Just because you're not an advertising professional, expert speaker, writer or motivator, don't think you can't advertise God every bit as well as the next person. It doesn't matter where you are on your faith growth line. Advertising God is something anyone from the neophyte Christian to those mature in his or her faith can do with great effectiveness. All you have to do is talk about someone you love who showers you with unconditional love. Someone who fills your life with an abundance of joy, hope, comfort and blessings. Someone who always hears and discerns your individual prayer from the millions who are simultaneously praying. Someone who is always there ready to forgive and restore. And if you still feel like you're not communicating the point, then let your Christ-first actions speak for you.

We love, worship and serve a truly awesome God. It's time to pick up your Cross and proudly give God His rightful due in front of others instead of hoarding your joy in Christ all to yourself. You can't assume someone else will be the one who does it either—advertising God, as you've seen, begins with you!

Unfortunately, we've all passed on a prime opportunity to advertise our faith at one time or another. Maybe it was the end of a long day, maybe you had someplace else to be, maybe you weren't feeling well or particularly inspired, maybe it seemed like too much of a hassle, or maybe you were guilty of prejudging and you just didn't think advertising God would have any kind of tangible effect on that person or group.

Missing a chance to advertise God happens to even the best and most faithful of Christians, but when it does, you may feel guilty, sinful and remorseful afterwards. That's probably because, deep down in your heart, you know you could have handled the situation better, and you really wish you had a second chance to prove it. You know you should have put forth a stronger effort, then spent the necessary time doing God's work. You know serving others in the name of Christ is what God wants you to do. But, if you're not careful, nothing changes day after day until pretty soon, you become callous, indifferent, and maybe even oblivious, to the very real and pressing need those who are without Christ have for seeing and hearing dedicated Christians like yourself advertise the benefits of our loving God.

Even for active Christians, the trappings of a passive attitude are easy to fall into and tough to get out of. That "do-nothing" attitude can be extremely frustrating, especially when you enthusiastically tell family, friends, neighbors, coworkers and acquaintances all about a positive experience you've had as a consumer in the marketplace, but remain silent when it comes to extolling the love and benefits God offers.

Something so seemingly simple—promoting and praising the awesome God we love so much with others around us—is something that's surprisingly difficult for many faithful Christians to do. And because of that pent up fear and passiveness, it seems many Christians would rather opt for a root canal or undergo a cavity search than share their faith with unbelievers or readily talk up their faith with real conviction to friends and coworkers outside the church. But it doesn't have to be this way, and I want to help you grow to where you feel more comfortable and confident sharing your faith. Besides, I've heard those root canals and cavity searches aren't all they're cracked up to be!

If advertising God is a real struggle for you, now is the time to start turning things around. Not tomorrow or next week, but today. It's time to start sharing your God-given talents and experiences with others so you and the ones you're sharing with can reap the full benefits of an abundant Christ-fulfilled life. As Christians, we have heavenly praise on our lips and in our hearts and we have the greatest of all news to share. Believe me, if you can talk up a good burger, the latest bestseller, a reliable plumber or anything else that generates excitement in your life, you can glorify God.

## Your "How-To" Manual for Advertising God

By using the techniques outlined in this book, you'll be able to overcome the obstacles and barriers that both the world and Satan throw your way, and you'll learn how to aggressively advertise God with spirit-filled power, enthusiasm and confidence. The disciple John reminds us in 1 John 2:17 that, "The world and its desires pass away, but the person who does the will of God lives forever." It's true God wants us to enjoy life and the world we live in, but if you're a slave to worldly pleasures and pursuits at His expense, it's time to redirect your focus and get back to the Christ-directed task of advertising God whenever and wherever you can.

With family, career, church and social responsibilities most of us juggle every day, it's not always easy to stand up and be the one God can count on. In other areas of your life however, you make time for things that are important to you such as volunteering at your child's school, dallying in your hobbies, starting an exercise regimen or coaching your child's baseball team. So be honest with yourself. If God is really that important to you, making excuses for not doing what He wants you to do is really lame on your part, isn't it?

God wants and even instructs us to put Him first in our lives in everything we do from tithing to prayer to reading and studying the Bible to getting involved in church-sponsored events and service projects. Instead of letting complacency and excuses control your life, let your life be ruled by God and revolve around Him. Making God your first priority every minute of every single day will free up time for you to pursue all the opportunities He puts before you. And, I'll bet you still find time to do all those other leisurely activities you enjoy, too! But, if not, serving God is about sacrifice.

As Christians, we are the ones charged with bringing the word and the light of Jesus Christ to the entire world. In advertising lingo, we are the catalysts, the ones promoting the love, fellowship and forgiveness of Christ to everyone we come into contact with as we live out our daily lives. Everything we say and do becomes a primetime commercial aired out daily and targeted towards persuading others to earnestly and enthusiastically accept Christ as their Lord and Savior. Like the old Nike ad slogan, Christ wants us to get out there and "just do it."

Remember, you are God's light to the world and Jesus instructs you in Matthew 5:16 to "let your light shine before men, that they may see your good deeds and praise your Father in heaven." Believers who are regularly called to advertise God are always on stage so to speak. Whenever you identify yourself as a Christian, there's going to be a brighter light that shines on you, and others will take note of your positive words and actions as well as your negative words and inactions. You have to be careful to always do what is right and Scripturally correct to ensure that you portray yourself and God in the best possible light.

And don't think you just have to advertise God to unbelievers—Christians need to see and hear you advertising God, too. Seeing and hearing you empowers and encourages them and they gain courage and confidence by follow your lead. So what are you waiting for? Get out there and make that light of yours shine!

## UP FOR DISCUSSION.

1.  What are areas in your life where you could improve on advertising God?

2.  Recall a time when advertising God had a positive impact on your life or another's.

3.  With your spouse or a friend, engage in role-playing situations to help build your confidence when advertising God.

4.  Why do you think advertising God is so difficult for so many faithful Christians?

# 2

## *The Great Commission and Advertising God*

○ ○ ○ ○ ○ ○ ○ ○ ○ ○ ○ ○ ○ ○ ○ ○ ○ ○ ○ ○ ○ ○ ○ ○ ○ ○ ○ ○ ○ ○

"Therefore go and make disciples of all nations…teaching them to obey everything I have commanded you."

—{ *Matthew 28:19-20* }

Advertising God is, I believe, one of the basic tenants of Christ's great commission found in the New Testament. While gathered with His brave and loyal followers on a Galilean mountain, Jesus commanded them to go preach the good news and make disciples of all nations.

Christ's words are not merely directed at the faithful few huddled there with Him prior to His ascension, but to all of His followers today. In one of His last recorded statements in Acts 1:8, Jesus reaffirms that very command by declaring "you will be my witnesses in Jerusalem, and in all Judea and Samaria, and to the ends of the earth." Yes, you! Little ol' you who might think you have no real talent, no real faith, nothing of real value to offer the Lord. But nothing could be further from the truth. You are created by God. You were made special before you were born and have been given unique gifts you can use to honor and glorify God.

Substitute the name of your hometown, state and country in the verse above and Jesus' directive becomes even more personal, even more meaningful. You and I have been empowered by the Holy Spirit to be a disciple of Christ not only in the places we live, but to the entire world as well. Notice that Jesus' words in the Great Commission and in Acts 1:8 are neither a polite request nor a friendly suggestion. Jesus' intent was never for us to selfishly keep His love and salvation message among ourselves—He wants us to share it with everyone whenever we can by whatever means we can. Today, we call this kind of outreach servant evangelism and it is one of the cornerstones of Christ's teachings.

Rev. David Walters, one of the former ministers in my church carries the interpretation of Acts 1:8 an extra step further. Because Jesus was a real man with real human limitations, He was confined to being in one place at one time. By giving believers the gift and power of the Holy Spirit, Christ enables us, as His far-flung army of believer messengers, to be in many different places at many different times. Like a TV or radio commercial broadcast over the airwaves and delivered to millions of homes or cars simultaneously, we too are able to communicate the same Christian message to many different people all at once. And similar to the corporate advertiser who pays for an ad spot on TV or radio, we just don't want our audience to merely see and hear the message we bring. We want to give those to whom we advertise compelling reasons and motivation to act on the message they see and hear.

## Advertising God to Six Billion People

In and of itself, Christ's Great Commission appears to be a daunting challenge, a seemingly impossible call to action. Because really, don't you think it's just a bit much asking us to make disciples of all people? After all, right there are over six and a half billion people[2] living in 192 countries[3] all over the globe!

In truth, God realizes this is a lofty goal none of us alone could ever realistically achieve, not so much due to a lack of love or commitment on our part, but to the sheer magnitude and logistical complexities involved in accomplishing such a mighty task. Even in this era of instant communications with cell phones, e-mails and text messaging, sharing God's message with the entire world is still problematic. So how do we advertise God and His message to all these people?

Before you get caught up in the enormity of the challenge, let me suggest that Jesus doesn't expect each one of us to personally convert thousands and thousands of people. Rather than taking the words of the Great Commission literally, I believe what Jesus calls each of us to do is share the good news of Christ however and whenever we can with as many people as we can by using all the talents and resources at our disposal.

That means if you teach, then teach or mentor children, adults or special needs persons in your church. If you're a musician, sing or play an instrument in a worship service. If you sign, translate sermons for the hearing impaired. If you've beaten an addiction, be a compassionate counselor for others mired in the grips of an alcohol or drug dependency. If you're a fundraiser, organize events in your community or workplace for worthy Christian causes and events. Plenty of opportunities exist and the possibilities for serving God are as endless as your imagination.

Regardless of who you are or how you do it, once you tell someone about Christ and they commit to following Him, the basic premise of the Great Commission is that, through the Holy Spirit, they too will tell someone, who in turn will tell someone else, and so on until Christ's message reaches everyone in your town, your state, your country, and ultimately, all around the world. What once started as an enormous challenge is now seemingly much more manageable when you break it down into smaller numbers and components.

## Focus on the Bigness of God, Not the Bigness of the Obstacle

I believe all of us have great ideas and worthwhile talents we can put to use for God, but so many of us are too easily defeated and give up before we even get going. When you focus on the gravity of the task or the potential pitfalls that lie ahead, you grow less confident in your ability to accomplish something and shift your focus from the bigness of God to the bigness of the obstacle. We mistakenly convince ourselves that one person can't make a difference, that it's too much of a challenge or ordeal, or that no one else will share the same passion and enthusiasm we do for a worthy project or Christian cause.

Don't fall for Satan's lies and trickery! Let God be your guide and inspiration as you pursue the work He puts out there for you to do. Many successful charity events and organizations including the American Cancer Society's Relay For Life, Habitat For Humanity, and the Susan G. Komen Breast Cancer Foundation began as the direct result of one determined individual who passionately believed their efforts would have a positive and significant impact on the lives of others. These ambitious visionaries were undeterred in their efforts to succeed and surrounded themselves with like-minded individuals who could help make the dream a reality. Just look at all these organizations have achieved since their inception and you realize how one person's efforts can profoundly affect and impact the lives of so many.

Woody Allen once said 80% of success is just showing up. I think that's the way it is when we show up ready and confident to advertise God. Just taking that first step is often the most difficult, but once you get going you'll find yourself rejoicing in the happiness and success God can bring you. Consider that many Christians feel called to do "something." They just don't know what that "something" is until they hook up with you or hear some of your ideas. Right now, there are plenty of people, some you know, some you don't, in your church, in your community, in your workplace, in your neighborhood, in your children's school, who would love to get involved in your project either as leaders or active participants. God answers their prayers by using you, a faithful and obedient follower, to provide the way, the means, the "something" they feel God has been steering them towards.

Once you stop focusing on the magnitude of the Great Commission and concentrate instead on what you as an individual can do with the help of God, you'll begin to see that one person can indeed make a meaningful difference in growing Christ's followers. Rather than allowing Satan to deceive you into doing nothing, trust Christ instead and let Him lead you into the service duty for which you are called. Step forward, boldly share your ideas and successfully live out the command of the Great Commission by advertising God with courage and confidence. You'll probably be very pleasantly surprised at how God uses your actions to incite the passion of other like-minded believers, inspiring them to climb onboard and get involved as they live out their own faith.

## Bringing Bibles to the World…Advertising God in Action

Take the story of traveling salesmen John Nicholson and Samuel Hill[4]. While sharing a room in a crowded hotel one night in 1898, both men discovered they were Christians. Later that evening, after reading the Bible and praying together, they discussed forming a Christian association for traveling salesmen. Their schedules, however, forced the new friends to part ways the next day before any ideas could be solidified. Unknown to them, God's hand was at work. After meeting up again the following year, the two salesmen renewed their talk of creating a Christian association, and subsequently, along with William Knights, founded the Gideons.

At one of the association's early meetings, someone made the bold suggestion that the Gideons place a Bible in every single hotel room in the United States so traveling men would always have a Bible to read. The challenge was accepted and in 1908, the Gideons delivered their first Bible. Twenty years later, the association had distributed one million Bibles. Today, according to their website, the Gideons place more than 59 million Bibles annually in hotels, hospitals, shelters and prisons in over 181 countries and in 82 different languages[5]. That's an astonishing 112 Bibles every minute!

From random encounter to lofty idea to seizing the opportunity God placed before them, these three men and their army of "silent witnesses" played a major role in introducing millions of people around the globe to the love, teachings and salvation grace of Almighty God. Just how effective are the Gideons' efforts? Some years back, a Fodors survey revealed that 23% of American travelers had read a Gideons Bible in their hotel room[6]. Talk about following the command of the Great Commission, that's advertising God with extreme passion!

## We Advertise God by Doing the Work He Commands Us to Do

Advertising God is more than just talking the talk. People also see God in you based on your actions and in the acts you do. For example, it's one thing to tell someone you'll pray for them. It's quite another to take hold of their hand, get down on your knees together and actually pray with them. Actions like that have a profound and lingering effect on people because it gives them a chance to see, experience and interact with the presence and power of the living God in you. It also demonstrates a caring and compassionate commitment to your faith.

But because such actions are not always easy or convenient, some believers consider Christ's Great Commission to be a laborious and intrusive chore, and they find sharing the Word vocally and physically to be an unpleasant, uncomfortable experience. Rather than faithfully affirm their love and commitment to Jesus Christ by obeying His commands, these people find it easier to retreat to the safety and comfort of their home or office and remain quiet about their faith. Or, they lose sight of God's goals because they get selfishly caught up in the day-to-day goings on in their own lives while chasing worldly happiness and pleasures. The servant's heart that God asks of His believers isn't fully shaped into what God wants it to be yet in them.

What does it take to develop and maintain a servant's humble heart? First, it requires a genuine commitment to put God first in your life. If you continually put work, social activities and leisure pursuits first, then give God any leftovers you can't expect to have a first-rate servant's heart. Step back and re-evaluate your priorities. Decide what's really important in your life and that of your family. Is it working overtime and building up a big fat bank account? Is it boating every weekend? Is it participating in after-school activities every weeknight? Is it season tickets to the ballpark? Or is it developing a personal relationship with Jesus Christ and focusing your life, your time, your energy and your money on Him first and relegate other things as secondary priorities?

We are all entitled to hobbies and recreations, so I'm not suggesting there's anything wrong with enjoying life and fun activities with your family. God absolutely wants us to enjoy life and blessings He has given us. Such healthy diversions only become an unhealthy problem when we devote more time, energy and attention to these things than we do building and strengthening our relationship with Christ and passionately pursuing the evangelical work He calls us to do. Worldly things come and go, but the love, power and joyful life we experience in

Jesus Christ transcends this world and lasts forever. You can't have it both ways—either you put Christ first and foremost in your life or you don't. And, trust me, it shows. People will take note of your priorities and passions and see through your transparency very quickly if your words and actions aren't in harmony with Christ's teachings.

I believe the vast majority of Christians have a very strong desire to put Christ first in their life. They want to do the right thing and abide by Christ's teachings. But we humans are a busy bunch and there are lots and lots of distractions that threaten to keep us out of church and away from the service work God wants us to do. If you struggle with this dichotomy, you know what I'm talking about. You work all day. You taxi the kids from school to ball practice to the video game store and back home. You clean house and cut the lawn. You exercise. You watch the big game on your new HD plasma TV. You make plans for a weekend dinner party. Distractions are everywhere. No wonder you're strapped for time and zapped of energy.

It's nothing new. Centuries ago, the apostle Paul wrote in Philippians 2:21 that "everyone looks out for his own interests, not those of Jesus Christ." Ouch. Reading that verse stings a little, doesn't it? Especially when you realize Paul could be talking about you. No devoted Christian purposely seeks to push Christ out of the way, but we've all been guilty of spiritual laziness and apathy at one time or the other. The point here is not to judge or criticize your lifestyle or the leisurely activities you enjoy, but to help you balance those things with a strong desire to continually express God's unfailing love as you strive to fulfill Jesus' command in the Great Commission.

## Is Your Comfort Zone a Little Too Comfortable?

When you advertise God, you have to begin thinking outside the protective confines of your close circle of friends and family. You have to learn to trust your faith instead of your intellect and reason. You have to learn to face down fear and take risks in the name of Christ. Some Christians are literally called for mission duty that requires them to go national or international, but the majority of us can effectively deliver God's message right in our own neighborhood, community and workplace. You can do this by praying or sharing faith stories as a family, volunteering for civic and church duties, leading a Bible study at your office on your lunch hour, and by decorating your home or office with items that say something about your faith. Just look around, there's no shortage of ways you can advertise God (check out 101 simple ways you can share your faith with others in Chapter 11).

No matter what you decide to do or how you decide to do it, remember that advertising God means getting out of your comfort zone and putting your faith into action. It means not getting bogged down by rules, regulations and routines that inhibit your relationship with Jesus Christ. It means separating yourself from the people and places that are detrimental to your faith and begin actively pursuing service opportunities that please God instead of living to please your friends, family, coworkers or fellow citizens. It means worrying more about becoming a faithful and humble servant and worrying less about what you want to do or what others will think or say about you when you advertise God.

## Go Where God Leads You

In Ephesians 5:1, Paul urges us to be imitators of God and live a life of love. Jesus wasn't worried about his reputation when he dined at Matthew's house with other tax collectors and sinners, challenged the religious scholars, showed compassion to the maimed and the sick on the Sabbath, or forgave lowly prostitutes. Neither should we worry about the opinions of others when we seek to do God's work.

Recently, I heard about a singles Bible study group that held its meetings at a Hooters restaurant in Atlanta. A chain of casual eateries where its young female servers wear tight, body-hugging tank tops and skimpy orange shorts, Hooters is not exactly the kind of wholesome environment one normally associates with being an ideal place to gather, study, pray and worship God. Not surprisingly, the Bible study group sparked a bit of local controversy when their story was publicized on the news. When the topic was discussed on a morning radio show the following day, some Christian critics who called in complained the group was compromising Godly values and acting irresponsibly. Other callers disagreed and felt what the group was doing was in harmony with Jesus' teachings. Supporters affirmed the positives of taking the Word of God to places where people who might not otherwise attend a traditional Bible study could go and feel comfortable reading, studying and discussing the Bible, even if it was over beer and hot wings.

I think Jesus would agree with the supporters' position. Advertising God isn't just about promoting Jesus Christ to the people we work with or those living in our neighborhood. It's about reaching out to the entire community, whether we like where they eat, drink and congregate or not. Jesus doesn't call us to judge the restaurant, the girls who work there, nor any of the customers who patronize it. He calls us to follow the command of the Great Commission and bring the word of God to all the people wherever they are. If that's a Hooter's restaurant, pool hall or jail cell, so be it.

God never promised that following the road of the Great Commission would be lined with bright lights, clean sidewalks and directional signs that point us only to the most comfortable and desirable places. Starting a Bible study in an unconventional location away from the church or worshipping with those we deem to be outside our social ranks is sadly perceived as a risky endeavor for those Christians who are far more concerned about their own status or reputation than they are about going where God's work takes them.

## Not a Perfect World, Not a Perfect People

As I've mentioned, most purpose-minded Christians want to lead a life that's pleasing to God, but all too often fall well short of His commands and expectations. Most aspire to follow His commands and do good things and can think of no higher compliment than to hear God proudly say to them one day, "Well done, my good and faithful servant." Unfortunately, because we are imperfect beings, we may find ourselves being guilty of spiritual elitism at times. That's because we want to stay close to home in familiar and safe places where we don't have to mingle with people we look down upon or that are different from us. For some, that means they wouldn't dare go to an inner city soup kitchen or volunteer a weekend working in a poor, rundown area doing God's service work. Again, you can't always assume someone else will go in your place. Without your presence, work may go undone or projects may be left uncompleted. Limit the places you're willing to go in the name of the Lord and you vastly diminish your capability to advertise God and to let God fulfill His love work through you.

If you're being completely truthful and introspective, you might also admit that you may have wrongly pre-judged those you think are worthy to receive God's word and those you believe are not. The sad truth is, persons who desperately need to hear us advertising Christ's message the most are most often the ones we tend to overlook the easiest—the lonely, the outcast, the addicted, the afflicted and the downtrodden. Many of them are physically incapable or too ashamed to come to church, or worse, they are made to feel unwelcome and unworthy. They may even be politely or not so politely discouraged from ever coming back. Some will unfairly judge them on what they are right now instead of the new person they can become in Christ. We wrongly assume they can't become effective followers and advertisers of Christ simply because of their past or current problems, they way they look or the way they speak and act. That kind of pompous and callous Christian behavior on your part blatantly goes against everything Christ teaches. Can you imagine Jesus turning someone away just because that person didn't fit the right mold or expectation? And what if someone in your church or community had labeled you as a misfit when you wanted to come to Christ? Where would you be today if that had happened and how would it have made you feel?

Remember, we all love and worship the same God and have the same goal—to spread Christ's message to as many people as we possibly can. Avoid pigeonholing those you think will be a worthy servant of Christ and those you think will not. You only have to look at Paul to see how a person can make a radical change from godless adversary to godly supporter. Other believers outside your social circle may very well do things much differently than you would, but Christ teaches us to support their efforts, not criticize and undermine their work or make them feel exclusionary. In Luke 9:49-50, the disciple John jealously tells Jesus he and the other disciples saw a man driving out demons in Christ's name. Jesus replies, "Do not stop him, for whoever is not against you is for you." Don't knock someone down for how they go about things—build them up instead! Once you come to understand and accept what they're doing, you might want to step in and lend a helping hand. Who knows? You may find new avenues, new allies and exciting new ways in which to carry Christ's message further.

## What Risks Will You Take for Christ?

Most Christians readily admit that it's considerably easier for them to advertise God when they are in a safe place surrounded by other like-minded believers such as in a worship service, Sunday school class or Bible study group. But, remove them from their comfort zone, and many of these same Christians may begin to feel strangely out of their element. Outside that place of safety where Godly allies stand firmly with them, these Christians become hesitant and either unwilling or unable to speak up for Christ because there's no reasonable expectation or assurance of the reaction they might receive. Fear gives way to silence, silence gives way to inaction, and another chance to advertise God slips by.

To be a true servant of Jesus Christ who lives for God with confidence and conviction, you eventually have to risk venturing out of your comfort zone. It's not easy at times, especially when you're outside of your church or when you're around people who may not share the same religious beliefs and values as you. You might feel like a fish out of water or a lamb surrounded by a vicious pack of snarling wolves, ready to be attacked the moment you speak your mind. One can imagine how Jesus felt when preaching to angry mobs that stood ready to kill him at a moment's notice, or the anxiety and trepidation Christ's disciples encountered as they traveled from city to city in hostile lands preaching, spreading the gospel and starting churches. Some of these early advertisers were berated with insults, pelted with rocks, jailed, even tortured and murdered for their Christian teachings and beliefs.

At some point, you too have to decide what kinds of risks you're willing to take in order to share your faith in Christ. Will you be one who lets fear and intimidation hold you back from advertising God? Will you be one who tames or alters Christ's message in order to avoid striking a nerve or stirring up a controversial issue? Or will you be the one who takes the Great Commission to heart and bravely, joyfully and willingly proclaims the good news of Jesus Christ anytime, anywhere and anyplace without fear, hesitation or compromise? Jesus tells us we cannot serve two masters. If you're always trying to please others by silently stepping back into the shadows of complacency or watering down God's message, you are not serving Christ to the best of your ability, nor are you serving Him in the ways He instructs you.

The next time you feel the urge to speak up in what you perceive is a not-so-comfortable setting, ask yourself what's the worst thing that can happen. Chances are, the hostile scenarios you fearfully envision will never materialize. For the most part, people will respect your beliefs and opinions even if they disagree. Sure, you may get a few snickers or insults along the way, but so what? Many modern day disciples in far less hospitable places around the world risk much worse suffering than that, yet willingly put themselves in harm's way to joyfully and faithfully promote the gospel and salvation message of Jesus Christ.

*Advertising God in Real Life:*

*Steve and Rachel sign their 8-year-old son Devin up for recreational baseball. At the team's initial parent/player meeting, Devin's coach tells the parents that due to the amount of teams participating in the league, some games are scheduled to start at 10:00 a.m. on Sunday mornings. Steve points out this schedule will interfere with church and asks if the coach would see if Sunday games could begin after 1 p.m. The coach says the schedule is finalized and cannot be changed.*

*Unconcerned with what all the other parents think or whether or not they agree, Rachel echoes Steve's concerns and boldly proclaims that in her family, nothing, not even baseball, comes before church, and on those Sunday mornings when games are scheduled, Devin would be in church, not on the baseball field. After the meeting, several supportive parents tell Steve and Rachel they agree with their position and express gratitude that they had the nerve to speak up for what they believed in.*

*Steve and Rachel advertise God by standing firm in their faith, not putting recre-ational activities before God, and by expressing their commitment to worshipping Christ in front of others.*

## Sell Them on God

In Christ's Great Commission, I believe we are all called to be salespeople for God. We all dearly love our "product" (God) and have opportunities every day to "sell" Him through our words, actions and deeds.

Although life isn't a 30-second commercial, we really do only have a limited amount of time to convince others that Jesus is the way to go in order to find real joy and fulfillment in a Christ-centered life. Corporate advertisers are fond of compulsory expressions such as "hurry, time is running out," "three days only," and "limited quantities available" that are used to hasten your buying decision. Unlike secular promotions that have a specific end date however, Christ's offer of salvation isn't a one time or limited offer. His gift is truly life's greatest deal because it is always available, and always available in abundant quantities.

Best of all, Christ's salvation is yours absolutely free because the wages of your sin have already been paid for when Jesus went freely and lovingly to the cross. The salvation He offers is eternal and never-ending and is yours for the taking 24 hours a day, 7 days a week, 365 days a year. You don't have to take a number, wait for a special promotion or discount, or need a coupon. All you have to do is step forward and claim it, then show others how to do the same as you begin to faithfully advertise God.

I've never been a fan of scare tactics as it relates to promoting and advertising God, but I do believe we should remind people who procrastinate making a deci-sion for Christ that, as loving, patient and compassionate as God is, Christ's offer does indeed have an expiration date and it terminates the moment you die. The end of life on earth is, in my mind at least, Christ's deadline for accepting or rejecting Him.

No one, of course, likes to think about death. That's why we postpone buying life insurance, writing a will, or buying a funeral plot. But, the reality is, every-one's time on earth will eventually expire and God's judgment will be upon those who don't come to Him. Some people just can't seem to come to grips with a spiritual certainty—that short of the Rapture, everyone will face death one day and stand before God. As a result, some will move accepting Christ to the back burner. In other words, they figure they have plenty of time to find Jesus.

In general, younger persons especially, rarely envision themselves growing old and gray. They live for the here and now. For them, time is their ally and oftentimes what can be pushed off until next week, next month, next year will be. Or, for those who truly revel in the sinful life and mistakenly feel like Christianity takes all the fun out of living, they figure they can wait to accept Christ just prior to death. Like the condemned thief on the Cross, they can come to Christ of course, but they'll never really know and appreciate all the real joys and countless blessings God could have heaped upon them over a lifetime of faithful service or the difference they could have made sharing their faith story and spiritual gifts with others.

How do you get someone to commit his or her life to Christ before the offer "expires?" I wish I had the end-all answer to that question. What I do know is that people need to come to Christ voluntarily with a repentant heart. Some come to Christ early in life, others accept Him later, and others, as we just discussed, wait until death appears imminent. There is no one-size-fits-all timeframe. It's much like making a purchasing decision. Advertisers usually can't force you to buy their product or service. It's up to each individual to make the decision to buy or not to buy. When they feel like it's the right time for them, they buy. Similarly, you can't force somebody to accept Christ. Everybody comes to Him in his or her own unique and personal way when the moment feels right.

But that doesn't mean we can't help nudge persons towards accepting Christ by praying for them, encouraging them, being a positive Christian influence, patiently befriending them however we can, and never giving up on them. In the end though, like the corporate advertisers pushing their wares, we can only do so much persuading. We can't be responsible with what they do with the message once they receive it. Ultimately, as I said, the final decision rests with the individual because God gives them this little thing called free will so they can make their own choice. In Matthew 12:30, Jesus teaches we are either for Him or against Him. No one can have it both ways. God leaves no room for indifference or indecisiveness. Either people accept the message of Christ and proclaim Him as their Lord and Savior or they reject Him. It's really that simple. If there's someone you've been after to accept Christ, pray like crazy for God to work through you or others to open up communication or a path by which they are lead to seek the forgiveness and salvation of Jesus.

## The "What If" Mentality—Don't Go There!

Advertising God should come naturally, but for many Christians, there's something that seems to hold you back. Maybe you feel like your tongue is glued to the roof of your mouth. Or your feet are mired in mud. Or your rear end is stuck to the chair. Maybe you're afraid of saying or doing the wrong thing. You're worried you might offend someone. You hesitate to volunteer because it conflicts with some of your leisure time. You definitely feel God's call to get into the game, yet you remain content to stroll safely along the sidelines instead where there are no expectations or requirements leveled at you. On the sideline, you can't be criticized, challenged or experience failure because you're not playing. For many Christians, it's simply easier to do nothing than risk exposing yourself to or dealing with all the negative "what ifs" that run through your mind.

I should know. I'm a not-so-proud owner of the "what if" mentality, and it usually rears its ugly head whenever I venture into areas that are unfamiliar to me or when opportunities come about and the outcome is uncertain.

In 1996, for example, I felt God calling me to write and direct a stage play. I confess right away that I am not a playwright, nor have I ever had any formal training in the theater. Although I've dabbled in creative writing throughout my life, I never had the inclination, much less the determination, to write a play. Still, God's call persisted.

But God, I said trying to reason with Him, I know nothing about dramatic theater. I don't know anything about scripts, sets, stage movement, timing and directing actors. I don't know if I'm really the right guy to do this. What if I can't pull it off? But God's call persisted.

So I accepted God's challenge and began writing. Much to my surprise, the story came together quickly, and within a few months, the play was nearly written. It was very exciting to see God's hand at work guiding the entire writing process. But as the momentum was building, the what ifs reappeared. What if the script was bad? What if I couldn't find any actors? What if this, what if that. I worried and stressed about it all. Still, God's call persisted despite all those negative thoughts.

Once the script was completed, I held a casting call and several members of the congregation showed up ready and very eager to participate. Roles were subsequently cast, walkthroughs and rehearsals were scheduled, and advertisements were made and distributed. Things were definitely looking up, until our last rehearsal before opening night.

That day many of the actors were out synch. Lines were forgotten. Cues were missed. Timing was off. It seemed all those what ifs I had fretted over were now materializing. I went home that night quite discouraged and more than a little worried that this play could turn into a big embarrassment. But deep down, I earnestly believed God wouldn't let us get this far only to have us fall flat on our faces. I prayed that night for a successful production of the play and left the rest up to God.

About fifteen minutes before the curtain came up the following night, I gathered the cast and crew in a circle. We joined hands, bowed heads and I started a prayer, again asking God to bless and guide the successful production of His play. To me, it really was His play, not ours. We weren't there for our glory, but for His. Others in the circle added their own prayers, and it was during this time that I felt the unmistakable presence of Christ huddled there with us. I could sense a rush of adrenaline and surge of confidence welling among us as the power of the Holy Spirit flooded the room. Calm and reassurance swept over me, and as the buzz from the capacity audience echoed from the sanctuary upstairs, I knew this play would come off flawlessly. And it did. Not because of all our efforts and collective talents, but because God gave each of us the courage, confidence and creativity we needed to succeed in His work. The what ifs had been defeated by the what can be power of Jesus Christ.

The entire experience taught me that God doesn't ask us to witness or do service work for Him, and then allow us to fail. If we find ourselves in a situation where we truly do fail, it's usually tied to our own shortcomings, our inability to put our total trust in God by letting the what ifs guide our decisions instead of God, or we simply flat out go against what God wants us to do. In other words, we bring failure upon ourselves.

One more thing about the negative influences of what ifs. I've learned over the course of my life that plenty of the what ifs I stress and struggle over usually never happen. Instead I end up wasting a lot of good energy worrying about nothing. So go on, let God lead you to new and exciting possibilities. You won't regret it. In fact, once you do it, you'll probably wonder why you waited so long to follow God into those unexpected places or tackle a task that once seemed too mighty to accomplish.

## Using the "F" Word

Faith. It's something you've got to have when you fully commit yourself to following God. You can't be wishy washy or half-hearted about it either. You have to grab hold of true faith and chase God's work with passion, determination and gusto. At some point, you have to ignore all the uncertainties in life and embrace and trust the faith you place in God to get things done. One little faith step may not seem like much, but once you realize God is there for you and that He can and will remove obstacles that block your path, each subsequent step gets a little bit easier.

With God, there are no boundaries, no limits, no impossibilities. In Mark 11:24, Jesus says, "Therefore I tell you, whatever you ask for in prayer, believe that you have received it, and it will be yours." Jesus' words resonate with authority and empowerment, and I fell in love with that Scripture the first time I read it. Harnessing the power of prayer is truly an awesome thing, and when you decide to faithfully commit yourself to advertising God, you can take full advantage of Christ's prayer promise in Mark 11:24. When you really believe the words in that verse and actively live them out, you affirm to God and to others that you will follow His lead wherever it takes you.

Naturally, it takes a strong leap of faith to make a statement like that to God. Because having genuine faith is often times like walking off a steep cliff and into the empty void of weightless air. You know it makes no sense whatsoever, but true faith means you step off that cliff anyway, knowing with absolute certainty that God's loving hand will be there to catch you and prevent you from falling. That's the kind of faith God wants us all to have. As the author of Hebrews writes in 11:1, "faith is being sure of what we hope for and certain of what we do not see." It's the kind of unwavering faith that moves the "mountains" in your path, cures an incurable disease and creates amazing opportunities that once seemed implausible.

God's lead may take you to some strange and dim places or allow you to accomplish things you never imagined possible. No the road isn't always smooth. There's going to be potholes and wrong turns along the way, but once you arrive at your destination, you realize the journey, that memorable, exciting trek from here to there, was well worth the trip.

It reminds me of when my brothers and I were kids on vacation at the beach. We loved to ride the incoming waves that rolled towards the shoreline. We would dash full speed out into the ocean, the inflatable rafts we clutched in hand skipping and flopping across the choppy waters behind us. As the white-capped waves curled and crested, we would hop aboard our rafts and ride those walls of water as far as they carried us. It's the same way when following Christ. Faithfully hop on your raft and let Jesus take you on the joy ride of your life!

By advertising God with confidence and authority, you position yourself as a faithful follower and servant of Jesus Christ, one who will help guide and inspire others to reach out for His redemption and saving grace. And that's what the Great Commission is really all about.

## UP FOR DISCUSSION.

1.  What role do you play in Christ's call in the Great Commission? How does the Great Commission define your life's purpose?

2.  Why is it easier at times to please people instead of God? Is there a way to strike a healthy balance between the two?

3.  What are some things you can do to make getting out of your comfort zone less stressful?

4.  Describe a time in your life when you felt God asking you to take a leap of faith. How did you respond?

5.  How does the "what if" mentality affect your ability to advertise God?

6.  Is there a right place and wrong place to advertise God? Discuss.

# 3

## *Business Principles and Advertising God*

o o o o o o o o o o o o o o o o o o o o o o o o o o o o o o o o o o o

"If you do not stand firm in your faith, you will not stand at all."

—{ Isaiah 7:9 }

In our society, there is nothing nobler than saving a person's life. Most of us have a built-in rescue mechanism that kicks in whenever we see a person in a potentially harmful or fatal situation. We tend to react proactively, blocking out danger and instinctively put our own lives at risk just to save another. No one would think of callously or indifferently watching as a person drowns or is in serious need of medical attention if we could do something to help.

It's the same way in the spiritual realm. If you see or know someone who isn't saved or is continuing to live in an unrepentant lifestyle, it is incumbent upon you to save that person from a spiritual death. Advertise God in a positive, persuasive manner to help them either come to know Christ, get reacquainted with Him, or help them reach out for God's merciful forgiveness. A few kind words may not be sufficient either. It may require you to take extra steps and spend some of your time, money and resources. Saving someone's life makes you a hero of the faith, especially when you combine your actions with some of the tried-and-true advertising principles of the corporate world to successfully advertise God.

Up to this point, I've focused on what advertising God is and how advertising God relates directly to Christ's final instructions in the Great Commission. Now, I want to show you how some of the time-honored principles used in corporate advertising can be used in conjunction with your prayer and discipleship to advertise God.

## Create a Sense of Urgency

For the most part, advertisers are an impatient lot and want to make the sale as quickly and inexpensively as possible. It behooves them to create a sense of urgency in order to expedite a purchasing decision and drive up sales.

Urgency is that emotional, sometimes subliminal, persuasion that causes you to feel like you must have the item being offered right this very instant. Whether urgency is spoken or implied, advertisers have a strong desire to elicit a positive and actionable response on your part. In other words, they want you to purchase while the message is still fresh in your mind. That's why you see and hear such urgent phrases as "Hurry, this offer won't last," "Sale ends at midnight tomorrow" and "Call in the next 10 minutes to receive your bonus gift." That's also why so many fast food commercials air around noon, six and during the late, late show. Restaurant companies want to capitalize on that urgent need to feed your stomach. Advertisers know the longer you wait, the less likely you are to purchase their product. Or worse, they fear you will purchase from a competitor later on.

As a Christian promoting God, you too must create some sense of urgency with your audience. People not only need to hear your message, they need to respond to it in some actionable way. Why the hurry, you ask? First and foremost, Jesus himself tells us to be watchful and prepared for His return. The rapture is a Biblical promise, not wishful thinking, and Jesus tells us He will come again like a thief in the night. And, not to be morbid or depress you, but no one knows with absolute certainty whether they will actually be alive from one minute to the next. Keeping that in mind, the single biggest mistake one can ever make is dying without first accepting Jesus Christ as their personal Savior. It's a mistake that lasts forever and can never be undone.

Forever, I think, is a difficult concept for even the wisest people to grasp. Forever is a word that seems so vague, so nebulous and kind of hard to fully comprehend. Because we are bound by the limitations of time in our everyday lives and have been taught that nothing lasts forever, we somehow feel there must be an end to forever somewhere down the road. It's like the number line. You know it goes on and on, but subconsciously, you think it has to end somewhere, right? But God is not temporary or fleeting like time. He is eternal, He is forever, and once the body dies and the soul is claimed, your destination to Heaven or Hell stands forever as well. There is a very real degree of urgency that Christians need to address in their own spiritual lives and when sharing their faith with others.

Another reason to instill urgency among those to whom you're advertising is that the more time that elapses between the hearing of your message and the acting on it, the less likely they are to respond to Christ. Life distracts them as they settle back into old habits, and complacency and procrastination start to choke out any sense of urgency initially inspired within them when you advertised God.

I grew up in a small Southern Baptist church where classic fire and brimstone techniques were commonly used in Sunday morning sermon topics to instill that get-out-of-your-seat-and-come-to-Christ kind of urgency. Every week, the pastor exhorted anyone who hadn't accepted Christ to do so right then and there. Not later that day, not tomorrow or next week, but this instant because you just never knew what could happen on the ride home, the next day at work or anytime before next Sunday. For an impressionable thirteen-year-old like me, that was pretty scary stuff. That kind of frightening language and imagery fostered an instant desire and a pressing need within me to heed one of those Sunday morning invitations. In all honesty, I initially accepted Christ that day more out of the fear instilled in me by the preacher than out of a humble, abiding and sacrificial love for God.

Although fear can be an effective motivator for accepting Christ, I'm not sure it's the best way to create urgency when advertising God. Think about it. Does God really want us to come to Him out of love or out of fear like I originally did? Rather than scaring someone with images of sudden death and the enduring agony of Hell, focus on the positive instead. To convince someone to come to church or learn more about Christ and His Word, try using more affirming words and persuasive phrases that convey real excitement and passion about a life centered in Jesus Christ

One way to emphasize the positives is by saying things like, "I wish you'd come to church with me. I know you would love hearing our minister preach. He's so energetic and inspiring!" Or, "Let me tell you how my family's prayers lead to a healing miracle from God." Or, "I know you enjoy rafting. Next month, my Sunday school class is planning a rafting trip and we'd love to have you join us." When you accentuate and hype all the good things about Jesus and the church, you come across as a lot less threatening and preachy.

Another reason this approach works is because people love feeling connected to something or someone with whom they share common interests. It makes one feel like it's easier to gain acceptance within the group. Take advantage of worship topics, recreational outings and social events to reach out to people and get them more involved and interested in all that Jesus Christ offers. It may not be much at first, but getting people involved just on the fringes of the church and its activities is better than them not being involved at all. Plus, it's a great way to keep persons exposed to the ministries of the church and to Christ's teachings on a regular basis.

This proved to be true in our church when a teenager who had recently accepted Christ shared his testimony with the congregation. He talked about how he started coming to the church's youth group only because his friends did. He liked how no one pressured him to read the Bible, urged him to repent, or tried to ram Christ down his throat. The kids and youth minister just let him hang out, have fun and be himself. Soon, he started paying more attention to what the other kids were saying about Jesus and how God was such a positive influence on all they said and did. So that teen, he picked up a Bible one day, took it home and started to read. He began to ask spiritual questions and consider what kind of person he wanted to become. After a few months, he accepted Christ on his own accord, not out of social pressure or some misplaced obligation to be like everyone else. And it all started because he was initially welcomed into the youth group with no strings attached and was subtly exposed to the joy of Jesus Christ living in others.

## Urgency Means Persistence

Urgency is also synonymous with persistence. You can't just invite someone to church or Sunday school or urge them to accept Christ one single time and leave it at that. It is human nature to balk at change and procrastinate about having to go through it, especially when that change is something new and unfamiliar or a situation in which there is some degree of aversion, hesitancy or apprehension. When people think they will feel uncomfortable or out of place, their natural tendency is to postpone the experience as long as possible. No one likes being the new kid, feeling like an outsider or going someplace where they might feel out of their element. In your own life, think of the times you went to a new school, started a new job, or visited a Sunday school class for the first time. Experiences like this can be stressful, even a bit intimidating. Most people like the security and comfort of being in a place where they feel like they belong, contribute and have some relevance. Be understanding and patient when you encounter this kind of hesitancy, but also be persistent in your reassurances and encouragement to help persons grow more confident and comfortable when coming into a new place or situation.

One final thing about urgency. Much like corporate advertisers have discovered, creating a sense of urgency doesn't always translate to immediate results. In direct mail campaigns, an advertisement is considered a success if it generates a mere 1-3% response rate. Let's put that low number in perspective. For every 100 pieces mailed, a company gets an inquiry from or makes a sale to only 1-3 people. In the catalog creative industry I work in, it's not unusual for retailers to mail out 300,000 or more catalogs to customers and prospective buyers so the response-to-sales ratio is proportionate. In your own home, consider how many pieces of "junk mail" you toss out daily without responding.

A similar thing happens when you advertise God. Some people will hear the message and disregard it. Others hear the message and remember it, but make no move to act on it. Some are interested, but aren't ready to make a decision. It's only that small percentage that will process and accept your message, then buy into it.

Don't let the 97% or so that don't respond discourage you from doing God's work. Instead, pray for them and ask God to speak to their heart or lead them into places and situations where they can continue to see and hear positives associated with following Jesus Christ. Direct mailers and cataloguers don't give up on their customers after one or two mailings and neither should you. A retailer may mail three or four of the same catalog in one season, especially around the holidays, but in an effort to prevent customers from throwing the book away, they disguise it with a different front cover to give their catalog a fresh look. This marketing method also works to keep their name and image in front of the customer a little longer. Likewise, you can be the persistent voice that periodically delivers the promises of God and keeps His loving message in front of people by creatively changing or shuffling your words and actions to keep it fresh and to keep God on their mind.

## Identify Your Target Market

A target market is simply described as anyone the advertiser wants to buy their goods or services. But it's not enough for a business to merely define a target audience; they must get to know the people with whom they will be establishing a buyer/seller relationship. It's the first commandment of marketing—know thy customer.

Like the savvy marketer, a good Christian advertiser will know and relate to those in their target audience, too. For Christians, a target audience can be their Sunday school class, persons in their Bible study, an unchurched family member or neighbor, friends of your children, stay at home Moms, a group of men on a weekend retreat, coworkers gathered at the lunch table. You get the idea. Your target market is basically anyone with whom you want to share your witness, converse with about God, or sharing information with about tithing, volunteering or worship opportunities.

Because everyone is different and reacts to different triggering mechanisms, knowing general details about your audience, or target market, such as their core faith beliefs and willingness to serve Christ, can help you successfully market God and maximize the impact of your message. Some will respond to benefits and rewards. Some respond to challenges and competition. Some react to vanity or personal improvement.

It's not imperative to know these things to effectively advertise God, but if you do, try and tailor a message that will resonate well with the group. Kids in the Sunday school class you teach won't react well to discussion questions, but action stories from the Bible shared in an engaging, interactive manner will generate their interest. A defensive or "preachy" approach won't play well with those hostile to you when you're espousing your Christian beliefs, but emphasizing the positives of the Christian experience could.

Although God's message never changes, we must be flexible enough to change our delivery as the audience and situation warrants; however, we must always maintain the Scriptural integrity of the message we're sharing. In other words, don't change or soften the truth of God's word just to pander to whims or feelings of your audience. God depends on you to deliver the truth no matter what you think the reaction will be. Old Testament prophets like Nathan, Elijah and Daniel risked their lives speaking God's message to powerful and arrogant kings who could have easily ordered the prophet's execution if they didn't like what he had to say. For the dutiful prophet, it would have been much easier and safer to tell the kings what they wanted to hear, but these brave men chose to obediently deliver the truth God instructed them to deliver whether the news was favorable to the king or not.

## Establish God's Unique Selling Point

In advertising circles, a unique selling point, or USP, is anything that differentiates one product, company or service from another for the purposes of gaining a competitive advantage. Some familiar USPs you might recognize are Wal-Mart's low prices, Cascade's sheeting action and Dawn getting grease out of your way.

I believe God has a unique selling point, too. But unlike secular businesses that seek to establish a uniform identity, God's USP will be different for everyone based on their individual perceptions, attitudes and experiences. God made all human beings unique—no two of us are ever exactly alike in the way we look, speak or think. And, because a relationship with Jesus Christ is so personal, we all have a different idea of what God's USP is based on our own spiritual experiences throughout life. Therefore, our notion of what makes God so wonderfully unique will perhaps differ, maybe ever so slightly, maybe quite sharply, from another's because we all experience and come to God in so many different ways, from so many different backgrounds and from so many different mindsets. You may share similar attitudes and beliefs with like-minded individuals or groups, but the USP you assign to God could be much different than the USP attributed by your spouse, your best friend, your children, even your own pastor or Sunday school teacher. It doesn't make your USP right or wrong. It is what it is—God's unique selling point according to you.

To prove this point, try a simple test. Ask everyone in your family, Sunday school class, Bible study group or office to write a short phrase they think best describes who God Almighty is. After everyone responds, share the answers with one another. It's a spiritually enlightening exercise that should reveal how differently people even in the same group perceive God's amazing power and grace. I think it also proves just how awesome God really is in that all of us can relate to Him on so many unique and extremely personal levels.

I have no way of knowing what you wrote or what you might write, but I suspect words such as love, salvation, grace, forgiver, eternal life and holy have either entered your mind or were written in your description. That's because when you say God's holy name or that of Jesus Christ, certain words automatically trigger association with the Deity. Words that have probably been engrained in your mind since you were a small child. To put it another way, you've been conditioned over the years to elicit responses or thoughts to certain words. While universally, God may be synonymous with love and forgiveness, individually, God may mean something much more personal and specific to you.

In the Bible, Jesus is referred to as Teacher, Master, Son of God, Son of Man, The Word and the Good Shepherd. Moreover, Jesus says He is the Way, the Truth and the Light. All these references give Christians many images to consider when forming their personal perception of God's USP. As proven by our simple test above, even though people will share similar viewpoints regarding God's USP, all of us will maintain individual perspectives and ideas about what makes God so great. Remember to test your perception of God's USP by making sure it is grounded in Scriptural teachings and principles. My mother always says Scripture interprets Scripture, and she's right. If you're not sure whether your beliefs and interpretations about God and His purpose are Biblically correct, pray about it, consult with your minister, or study the Bible for verses that support your beliefs.

It's important to reiterate that there is no right or wrong USP for God, assuming the criteria mentioned above is met. Because a relationship with Jesus Christ is so personal, it's entirely possible that you may even come up with several USPs, all meaningful, all valid and all rich in spiritual truth.

Naturally there are universal truths about God and Jesus Christ that every Christian believer must honor and abide by, but it's how you allow God to lead, guide and shape your life that helps you determine His USP. As we did in our test, start by thinking up adjectives and superlatives that best describe God. Think about God's direct impact on your life. Consider everything that makes God mighty and good. Think of why you worship and praise Him.

For many of us, God's USP is a no-brainer that comes to mind right away. Others may need time to think, decide and pray about it. Either way, determining your own interpretation of God's unique selling point will help you joyfully accept and appreciate all that God has to offer. And, trust me, this understanding will show through to others whenever you advertise God.

Emotion, too, plays as much a role in our perception of God's USP as does spiritual knowledge, maturation and life experiences. For someone who has endured grief and tragedy, God's USP may be defined as healer, counselor and comforter. If you've been abundantly blessed, God's USP may be that He is a rich provider. Maybe the familiar children's blessing that begins "God is great, God is good" inspires your USP. Or maybe God's USP is culled from the hymn *Jesus Loves the Little Children* or some other favorite music you sing. Some people also draw upon Scripture, sermons and ministry for their USP inspiration. And your USP doesn't have to remain unchanging. The things you find so appealing about God in your teens and twenties may change as you age and as certain events occur in your life.

Conversely, those bitter about a job loss, a deteriorating family life, a lingering illness or any number of other spiritual frustrations may apply a more negative connotation to God's USP. They find it more difficult to hone in on God's USP at this time because of all the negative forces swirling about them, and sadly, instead of drawing closer to God and relying on His steady presence and comforting reassurance to lift them up from sorrow and despair, some will actually retreat from God and blame Him for their misfortunes.

Whether you're going through good times or bad, always focus on the positives of whom God is and what He can do. Don't allow unpleasant circumstances and situations in life to cloud your perception of or quell your enthusiasm for advertising God. Our Christian character is born out of the events that shape our lives and by how God guides us through all the joys and comforts us through all the heartaches that come our way.

## Plan Your Strategy

Unlike the way it's sometimes depicted in movies and on TV, ingenious and successful advertising is not born from one of those ingenious moments where a character that's put on the spot conceives a brilliant ad slogan or campaign in a few seconds. In the real world, businesses and their ad agencies spend large amounts of time, energy and money considering, rejecting and re-considering the very best way to describe and position their products and services in the marketplace. Pondered are such things as product description and benefits to the end user, consumers who will use their product, evidentiary support for any claims made, and the most effective marketing vehicles and mediums in which to deliver the sales message.

When you advertise God, take a moment if you need to and pray and focus on the ideas you want to communicate most. Plan your message accordingly, and then tailor it to suit the personality and nuances of your target audience. The message is best when it's clear, concise, easy to follow and even easier to understand. Remember in 1 Corinthians 14 where Paul points out the futileness of speaking in tongues if there's no one who can interpret it? It's kind of the same thing when you deliver your message. If it's vague, convoluted and difficult for the average person to comprehend, you didn't do anyone much of a service. On the other hand, message formats that galvanize conversation, stimulate questions and encourage interaction will work exceedingly well, especially in a group setting.

As I said earlier, advertising God isn't always rehearsed or planned out in advance. Most of the time advertising God is spontaneous. And that's a good thing! You meet a new neighbor who inquires about a good church. You're with a client who makes disparaging remarks about God or asks about your faith values. You overhear the person in the airplane seat beside you talking on their cell phone and obviously struggling with a question about God. You're asked to say the blessing at the company picnic or Christmas party. These kinds of situations happen regularly. Because you never really know when and where these situations will play out, you can't plan or rehearse for them, and even if you do, the words and thoughts never seem to come out as perfectly as you intended. If you're like me, such spontaneity causes an unsettling fear of saying or doing the wrong thing. Because you haven't had time to plan and think through what you want to say and do, it's sometimes easier to not risk the embarrassment or chance coming across as sounding foolish. And when you recede back into silence, you miss out on still another chance to advertise God with that persuasive conviction you feel inside.

You can't really expect that God will always give you ample time to prepare a message when an opportunity to advertise Him arises. I think God puts people directly in your path so you can witness to them, so you can invite them to church, so you can partner with them on a service project, so you can offer rational Christian wisdom. For all you know, your lone Christian voice, no matter how demonstrative, absurd or insignificant you perceive it to be, could be just the one someone needs to hear at that very moment.

Never underestimate God's ability to get His message into the lives of those He wants to see or hear it. The message, whether planned or unplanned, could be a real life-changer for that individual, or at the very least get them to rethink their position about God and His role in their life. So again I say, don't give into your fear and let another opportunity pass by without saying or doing something positive for God!

## Set a Goal

From an early age, we are taught to set goals for ourselves. Goals give us something to aspire to, a benchmark to reach or exceed. We strive for straight As in school, work hard to achieve a promotion, and save money for a comfortable retirement. Goals are constantly modified and tweaked as we age and as our wants, needs and ambitions change. Reaching a goal is a milestone and viewed as an indicator of success.

Advertisers set specific goals or threshold indicators to get an effective measure of how well an ad performed with the target audience. Defined parameters may include planned objectives such as increasing store traffic by 20%, raising revenues by $5 million annually, or creating greater awareness of a new product in the highly coveted 18-44 age demographic.

While many Christians religiously set goals in other areas of their life, they fail to set goals in their Christian faith. Ask most Christians what their spiritual goal is and they'll likely tell you it's to live a good, faithful life and get to heaven. That's a noble goal alright, but one that barely scratches the surface of living and serving out a Christ-centered life. Merely accepting Jesus Christ as your Savior, booking your reservation in Heaven, then coasting through life doing nothing meaningful for Christ is not what God intends for His followers to do. The apostle James tells us in his Gospel that faith without deeds is dead. So what does your faith say about you? Are you alive in Christ or dead in the spirit? Are you enthusiastically putting your faith to work for Jesus Christ or merely groaning through the motions whenever you're asked to do something for the church and its ministries?

You ought to be frequently setting Godly goals and praying you can successfully attain them. One of the easiest goals you can set is asking God to give you at least one opportunity every single day in which to advertise or share your faith. And when He does, follow through on it. Maybe it's a good deed done in the name of Christ, befriending an at-risk teen or offering an unsolicited response to someone's opinion or question about God. The opportunities to advertise God are abundant in your church and community. Learn to recognize the avenues God opens for you, and then take advantage of the moment. Challenge yourself to set those God goals on a daily basis and use your accomplishments as a measuring stick of your faith and your commitment to following the teachings of Jesus Christ.

*Advertising God in Real Life:*

*Beth and her husband Greg live in a quiet, middle class suburban neighborhood. One day, Beth watches as a new family moves into the house down the street. She notices they have children about the same ages as her own kids and feels like she has an "in" by which to introduce herself. Later that week, Beth bakes a cake, walks it down to her new neighbors and introduces herself to the new homeowner Susan.*

*Beth and Susan become fast friends and begin walking together every morning after the kids get on the school bus. One day, Beth casually asks if Susan and her husband Nick go to church. Susan says they try and that their intentions are good, but they usually don't make it.*

*"Not to pressure you or anything," Beth continues, "but Greg and I go to a great church. They have a fantastic young minister, really good musicians and there's always fun things going on that your kids can get involved in."*

*Susan seems uneasy and confesses that she's never really been able to commit to church and that they all like to sleep in on Sunday mornings.*

*"Come just once and I promise you'll be hooked," Beth pledges. "We just love it and I know you and your kids will too. It really is awesome. They have worship services and Sunday school classes that start later in the morning so you guys can still sleep late. Let me give you the website address so you can check it out for yourself."*

*Susan shrugs and says now that they've settled in, it might be time to make a real effort to give church another try. "And at least, I'd know someone there, too," she laughs.*

*"And I'm going to keep on asking until you decide to come with us," Beth declares with a smile.*

*Beth advertises God by casually, enthusiastically and persistently inviting a new friend to church.*

## Believe What You Say and Know the "Product" You're Promoting

People quickly see through masquerade, half-truths, double talk and unenthusiastic rhetoric. If you're excited about God and the promise of eternal life, others will get excited about Him, too. To be an effective advertiser of God, it is imperative you believe and embrace everything you say about Him and live your life in such a way that supports your beliefs. It's the classic cliché—you have to walk the walk and talk the talk in order to establish and maintain credibility.

Many celebrities who endorse products won't even consider becoming a spokesperson until they've had a chance to use and review the product or service for themselves. And who can blame them? No one wants their name associated with some poorly made or cheesy product that doesn't deliver on its promises. Sure, some less scrupulous pitch persons will lend their name just to make an extra buck or two, but the enthusiastic salesmanship they feign proves ineffective because the audience knows they really don't believe what they are saying.

It's the same way with Christians who advertise God. You can't expect to go out and promote God with any kind of real conviction if your whole heart is not in it. If you're like the celebrity who isn't convinced the product he or she is endorsing is really worthwhile, you come across as passive, dull and disinterested in the Almighty God you're selling. Do this and you're not giving an unbeliever any good reason to "buy" into the message and life-changing redemption of Jesus Christ.

Think about the overly aggressive car salesman who is far more interested in a quick sale and pocketing his commission than patiently listening to your needs, answering your questions and providing the best solution. It doesn't take long before you pick up on his insincerity, tune out all his hype, and walk out of the dealership. For first time car buyers, this type of salesperson has the potential to sour you on the whole car buying experience.

Maybe it's like that for the unsaved and the unchurched. Perhaps they've been to church, visited a Sunday school class, talked with a Christian believer, or participated in a church-sponsored event and came away feeling like Christians weren't really the kind of devout and pious people they claimed to be. Sure, these Christians talk about Jesus a lot, but the ways in which they live their lives and adhere to Biblical principles are in conflict with one another. Their duplicity and hypocrisy has the potential to turn believers off and sour them even more on the whole Christian experience.

Counteracting all this negativity, many Christians diligently devote time to prayer, spend time reading and studying the Bible, and regularly offer assistance within the church and on mission projects. These Christians have an active relationship with God and are excited to promote all the benefits He offers. When they advertise God, they speak with confidence and authority and come across as action-oriented Christians ready to promote God whenever they get the chance.

On the other hand, those who don't spend the necessary time cultivating and growing their relationship with Christ cannot advertise God with the integrity and credibility needed to persuade others that a life in Christ is really the only life worth living. Their lack of commitment, faithfulness and Biblical knowledge communicates an insincerity and unwillingness to go the extra mile. The unsaved figure that if you as the Christian don't bother with these things, why should they? Or worse, you send a message that it's okay to be passive about prayer, worship and obedience. Don't give non-believers and those straddling the fence another reason to tune out Christ's message. Do whatever it takes in your own life to ramp up your desire and enthusiasm to share God's word with others.

## Deliver on Your Promises

For Christians to be effective advertisers and agents of God, we must do what we say we will do. It's that simple. Nothing erodes confidence and undermines your credibility faster than half truths and broken promises. Consistently failing to do what you say you're going to do or making false and insincere promises is as much the kiss of death for a business as it is for the Christian advertising God. After awhile, people will tune you out and ignore your message altogether. How many times have you been to a store to buy an advertised item only to be told it's out of stock? Or been promised someone would be out to your house between 9 and 11 a.m., only to have them show up hours later if they show up at all? Or been told someone would call you right back, then doesn't? Remember how angry, frustrated and disappointed it made you feel? That's how others feel when you don't follow through on what you say.

When advertising God, we're selling and representing someone who never breaks His word and never fails to deliver on a promise. God is the ultimate promise-keeper. He is the way and the truth, and we must follow His lead. If God gives you an opportunity, thank Him for giving you the privilege of glorifying and praising Him in front of others. Let Him know you feel honored to do His work. Don't sit back and think of excuses why you can't say or do something—seize the chance God puts before you, then go out and enthusiastically do it in the name of Christ! If it's teaching Sunday school, teach. If it's serving meals in the soup kitchen, serve. If it's counseling youth, counsel. If it's praying for a person in need, pray. Make your word as dependable as your works. You don't like to hear excuses from companies you do business with, so don't make excuses with others who count on you in a time or area of need.

## Lead, Don't Mislead

Advertising is deceptively clever in the images and language used to persuade you. We've all seen those notorious before and after photos of the successful dieter and viewed them with skepticism. We've also watched those late night real estate infomercials where the host and all the amazingly "successful" guests try and convince you you'll be on the road to financial freedom with virtually little or no effort.

As a Christian witness, you have a responsibility not to convey misleading information when advertising God, even if the truth hurts or God's message is deemed to be politically incorrect. When advertising God, it's easy to get swept up in the emotion and tell people what they want to hear rather than what they need to hear. But, like the ads that leave you feeling distrustful, skeptical and wary, so too will people come to view you and Christianity in general in the same bad light if you aren't entirely truthful in your proclamations and explanations about God. If you're not certain of a Biblical truth or an interpretation of Scripture, be honest about it. No one knows everything. Let them know you'll get the answer for them or point them to a place where they can discover the truth on their own.

When trying to get someone to devote himself or herself to Christ, you also must be extremely careful not to perpetuate the myth of the perfect life syndrome or that life will somehow be a cake walk now that they've entered into a relationship with Jesus. While one's eternal life is certainly secure after accepting Jesus Christ, there's absolutely no guarantee that anyone's life here on earth will get any easier, that their problems will instantly disappear, that their bank account will grow fatter, or that they'll always be healthy.

The truth is, God never guarantees us a life filled with joy and only joy. He wanted things to be that way at the beginning, but the sin of Adam and Eve ensured life could never again be so utopian. Christians are no more exempt from health problems, layoffs, divorce, drug dependencies, depression, physical pain and heartache than anyone else. The difference is, however, we worship and believe in an active and participatory God that we can prayerfully turn to at any time to guide us through the rough times and bring us through. Perhaps not unscathed, but He still brings us through. How many times have you heard someone's tragic testimony only to find they consider themselves blessed for all the pain and agony they endured because it drew them closer to Christ?

All it takes is one read through the Bible to prove life is anything but perfect for even the most heralded of believers. Many faithful and obedient prophets and disciples never had an easy road in life. Paul had a physical affliction and spent time in prison. Stephen was stoned. David grieved when his rebellious son Absalom was slain. Mary witnessed Jesus' execution. Peter was physically beaten and crucified. Yet, despite their sufferings and sadness, all continued to love, praise and worship God.

For reasons unknown to us, bad things do happen to good people, Christians and non-Christians alike. It doesn't mean God loves those who prosper more than those who suffer. We all get sick. We all lose jobs. We all lose loved ones. The difference is Christians have a Lord who knows suffering personally and can help heal and restore us.

I believe the grace and healing power of Jesus Christ is available to everyone, and that even the most dire health circumstances can be remedied by God should He choose to do so. Like the Roman centurion who sought healing for his child, I believe if Christ just says the word, waves a finger, nods His head or whatever it is He does, His will is done, whether divinely through the Holy Spirit or through the intervention of a doctor and/or medicines.

I also realize that, for reasons known only to God, not everyone is healed or rescued from a bad situation. Who knows exactly why innocents suffer, why children get sick, or why one home is destroyed by a tornado while a neighbor's place is spared. God is not the author of tragedy, illness and calamity, but He is the one who can rescue us from it. And while you can't make promises of what life has in store for others or yourself here on Earth, the one promise you can make with absolute conviction is that, as a believer of Jesus Christ, you and all the others who follow Him will find eternal life in Heaven. Whether you've suffered or know ones who have, remember that we are all generously blessed because of God's infinite and unconditional love and His gift of eternal life.

## Focus on the Benefits, Not Just the Features

Regardless of what product or service a company is selling, inevitably the consumer wants to know "what can it do for me?" Let's face it, a product can have all the best features in the world, but if people can't see how all those great features benefit them, it's no sale. Think about this way. You see an ad for a new dishwasher. You know its features—computerized display pad, thousands of powerful jets, whisper quiet operation. This nice new machine sounds impressive enough, but if the features are tied to a direct benefit, it helps close the sale. For example, you learn the computerized display makes the dishwasher super easy to program, that thousands of powerful jets clean even the dirtiest of dishes, and it's so quiet you barely know it's running. Now that you better understand how the features of this particular dishwasher can help in your kitchen, you buy it.

Lots of people know God has plenty of great features like the ability to heal, the power to forgive sins and the love to guarantee eternal life, but inevitably, unbelievers or those skeptical of Christ want to know one thing—how can accepting Christ as their savior benefit them? In other words, they ask, "What is it that God can do for me?"

Help them answer that question by showing them how God's features, including the ones mentioned above, can directly benefit them. Got an addiction? God can help them kick it. Experiencing the loss of a loved one? God can give them peace. Got financial problems? God can help find a way out. Need encouragement in discipleship? God can provide the inspiration. After embracing Christ, the new believer's attitude will hopefully shift from the selfish "what can God do for me" mentality to the more humble and appropriate "what can I do for God."

## Guarantee God

Guaranteed or your money back. Satisfaction guaranteed. Lowest prices guaranteed. All these phrases are popular advertising terminology. Companies know that consumers feel more comfortable and empowered if some sort of guarantee exists. A guarantee implies quality, honesty and goodwill. A guarantee is a pledge from the retailer or manufacturer that you, the customer, will be taken care of. As wonderful as most product guarantees are however, none comes anywhere close to equaling God's ultimate guarantee as proclaimed by Jesus Christ in John 3:16 and reiterated by Paul in Romans 10:9-13.

But there is an interesting similarity between product guarantees and God's. Many product guarantees require certain conditions before the guarantee goes into effect. So it is with God's guarantee. God requires that something happen in exchange for His guarantee. The something happening is us believing in and accepting Jesus Christ as our Savior. The guaranteed promise is we will not perish, but have everlasting life. Some products even come with a lifetime guarantee. But God does their lifetime guarantee one better by giving us an even longer lasting guarantee that never changes, never wavers and never expires. Talk about the mother of all guarantees, God's eternal one is definitely it!

While God offers no guarantees about how your life on earth will go, His assurance of eternal life is absolute and certain. In Revelation 21:4, God promises us a place where "there will be no more death or mourning or crying or pain, for the old order of things has passed away." When things go bad in life, it never hurts to be reminding yourself or others of God's eternal guarantee. Like a product guarantee, God's offers comfort, peace of mind and reassurance that everything's going to be all right and that you'll be taken care of. Maybe not in the here and now, maybe not even down the road, but in heaven.

## Don't Minimize or Exaggerate God

Advertisers are fond of hyperbole, or exaggeration. You only have to watch the commercial of a pickup truck pulling a 20,000 ton submarine, see an inverted car hugging the roof of a tunnel, or hear a radio commercial describing a giant pink elephant slaloming down a candy-covered mountain slope on the latest and greatest brand of skis.

Hyperbole may be a great way to make a point in secular advertising, but when you're in the business of selling God, you don't need exaggeration or gross overstatements because God can do all things, however improbable they may be. Although the laws of nature established by God make some events unlikely, have no doubt that God can change the rules anytime He wants.

For proof, you only have turn to the Bible and read how Peter walked on water, how Jesus instantly healed the sick and the physically afflicted, how He feed 5,000 people from just a few fish and some bread, and how He raised Lazarus and others from the dead. All these events defy the natural order of things and appear to be seemingly implausible if not impossible from our limited human perspective. But events such as these, and ones we can't even imagine or even fathom, are absolutely possible with God. Remember Philippians 4:13? It affirms you "can do everything through Him who gives [you] strength." Sometimes, "all things" can seem far too insurmountable for us to overcome, but know that with God on your side there's nothing you can't do no matter how improbable it appears.

Alternatively, some secular ads try to minimize a company's achievements or endeavors through self-deprecation. As a Christian advertising God, you should never trivialize or attempt to explain away God's miraculous accomplishments in order to rationalize these events in your own mind or to placate others. Remain true to your beliefs and Biblical assurances in the face of opposition. You don't always have to understand how God did something or why He did it to become a faithful and influential witness. Embrace and acknowledge God's awesome power in the presence of others even if you don't always have all the answers.

## Follow Up After the Sale

You've done everything right. You've advertised God, been persistent in inviting that friend, neighbor or colleague to church, and they're now ready to accept Christ and claim their place in His eternal kingdom. Most of us would say mission accomplished and move on. But, now is not the time to abandon the new believer. Instead, you or those you designate should spend even more time nurturing them by praying, answering questions, sharing the Bible and worshiping with them.

You know all too well evil forces, temptations and distractions are out there trying to weaken a Christian's resolve and thwart God's plans. Like a company that has lost your business, but is aggressively wooing you with offers and incentives to return, Satan, too, has a relentless marketing plan that he will deviously use to reclaim those who once belonged to him, but now are struggling to stay with Christ. Satan doesn't like losing "customers" to God anymore than a company that loses your business to a competitor.

As a fisher of men, you can't allow the newest Christian believer in your church to suddenly become the one that got away. The road in the walk with Christ is fraught with pitfalls for everyone, but it's especially dangerous for those in the infancy of their beliefs. For them, a new life in Christ is as delicate as fine crystal and can be easily shattered. They need a mentor, a loving compatriot in Christ to help them strengthen their belief, empower their faith and reaffirm their resolve to repent especially during trying times when they're tempted to settle back into their old ways.

Think of those Sunday mornings when you witnessed a fledgling Christian professing his or her newfound love and devotion to Jesus Christ, and then join the church to great applause from the congregation. Maybe you're one who goes up after the service, shakes their hand and wishes them welcome. But how many Christians are willing to go the extra step, put an arm around the new believer and let that person know with real sincerity they'll be there for them whenever they have questions, whenever they stumble, whenever they experience a life crisis or whenever their faith falters or wanes? If we don't do this, it's like inviting a new friend to a party, then leaving him or her all alone to fend for themselves the rest of the night. It is hard enough to ward off Satan's advances even when you've been faithfully living out the Christian life for a long time. Imagine, then, how difficult the challenge is for new Christians who may not as yet have the spiritual strength, Biblical acumen or steadfast faith it takes to mount a successful defense against the volleys of worldly desires and temptations Satan hurls their way.

Like a mother protecting her young from potential dangers, we too have an opportunity, an obligation really, to embrace new believers and help mentor them in the early stages of their faith journey. I'm not saying you have to be a mother hen and never let them out of your sight. But, you should be proactive, genuinely letting them know you are there when they need you. And if they should call upon you, remember your promise and come to their aid. It takes more than token words to convey your devotion to them. It takes action. Just like you rely on God and expect Him to help you, let that new believer know he or she can count on you to come through even when it's not convenient or comfortable.

But why wait until they come calling or until the situation is dire? Like a good salesman tending to his customers, check in with the new believer every so often to see how things are going and if there's anything you can do for them. E-mail them inspirational quotes, Scripture passages and devotionals you run across to help lift them up and reinforce their decision to follow Christ. Offer encouragement by sending them a religious book that helps to solidify their belief and faith. In the business world, follow up is called good customer service. In the spiritual world, follow up is called shepherding the flock. Just as Jesus watches over us, so too should we follow the example of Christ and keep a watchful eye on those we invite to follow Him through the gate.

Unfortunately in the hustle and bustle of daily life, all too often a new believer is left to fend for himself and soon becomes like a ship adrift in rough seas. He wants to see the storm through, but sin and temptation are threatening to sink him. Without an experienced captain to guide him safely through these early storms, the euphoria of accepting Christ and joining the church can rapidly begin to fade. The new believer is more susceptible to Satan's follies than ever before and can easily revert back to the old habits and lifestyle he was once so determined to leave behind.

When you advertise God after the "sale," you become the friend, the mentor, the shoulder to cry on, and the one who can always be counted on when needed. It's not an easy role to take on, and there's a fine line between showing care and concern and becoming a nuisance. Try borrowing a page from our friendly car salesman's notebook. To stay in touch, he may casually contact his clients periodically by phone, mail a postcard every so often, or send birthday and Christmas cards. He's not being intrusive, he's subtly reiterating that if there's something you need, then he's the guy who is going to help you out.

While many Christians agree shepherding the new believer is the right thing to do, many are reluctant to do so. Maybe they worry it could take a lot of time and energy, that there could be personality conflicts, or they simply don't want to get that involved in another person's life. Christians can't afford to adopt this kind of attitude at all or we risk losing fledging believers back to the enemy.

Think back to your early days as a Christian. Remember the excitement of accepting Christ and getting involved in church and community ministries? But do you also recall the struggles you had steering clear of your old ways and the frustrations you had when life took a turn for the worst? Aren't you glad you had a loving Christian parent, friend or someone who cared enough to stick by until you grew more confident and secure in your faith? Or maybe you didn't and wish now that you had had that kind of person available for you. Someone you trusted to point you to specific passages in the Bible, lend a friendly ear when you needed to talk or simply take your hand and pray with you.

If you feel shepherding is one of your spiritual talents, don't pass the buck and walk away from the job. Christ needs you. The new believer needs you. If you're not gifted for shepherding, and all of us won't be, that doesn't give you an excuse to duck the responsibility. You can still help by directing the new believer to his or her pastor, a Christian counselor, a good Bible study group or Sunday school class, or to someone you know who can address his or her specific need or concern. They've come a long way. Don't let them get this far, and then fall away from God. Do everything you can to help. God will definitely smile upon you for doing it.

## UP FOR DISCUSSION.

1.   What are some ways you can get to know your "target market?"

2.   Define God's USP as it relates to your own understanding of who He is and your own life experiences.

3.   What goals do you have as a Christian? How do you plan to achieve them?

4.   Who helped mentor or guide you in the infancy of your salvation? How important were their prayers, influence and advice? Consider looking them up and letting them know where you are in your faith walk and express thanks for all they did for you early on.

5.   In what ways did Satan try to woo you away from God and back into a sinful lifestyle?

# 4

## *Get Creative Advertising God*

o o o o o o o o o o o o o o o o o o o o o o o o o o o o o o o o

"He who unites himself with the Lord is one with Him in spirit."

—*{ 1 Corinthians 6:17 }*

For as long as there have been buyers and sellers, there has been some form of advertising. In its earliest forms, advertising was primarily word of mouth. Later, advertising capitalized on the popularity of newspapers and magazines and found a much larger market to which it could peddle its wares. In the 20th century, as the industry grew more savvy and sophisticated, advertising took advantage of ever-changing innovations and technology to become the powerful force we now experience in some way, shape or form every single day. And while advertising's looks, contents and mediums have changed dramatically over the years, the core message has effectively remained the same. It's the familiar "my product or service is better than the other guy's, and let me tell you why so you will buy from me instead of them" marketing technique.

Today, you don't have to look far to see that advertising is a persuasive and pervasive force in our society. Like it or not, corporate advertising exists for one simple reason—it works. American business spends billions of dollars advertising their products and services every year. In fact, it's not unusual for giant corporations to have annual advertising budgets of $100 million or more. Advertising agencies and media buyers spend millions creating, printing and airing campaigns. Careers are made on ads that are memorable and successful and lost on those that aren't. Consultants and analysts are paid handsomely to dissect and analyze every aspect of a company's marketing plan to examine what works, what doesn't and what can be improved upon for the next campaign.

No wonder there's such a fuss over every ad produced. Factor in the cost of creative talent, production/studio expense and media placement, and it's not

49

cheap to advertise, especially on a hit TV show or in popular magazines. Placing a misplaced or misdirected ad can cost millions in potential lost sales and revenue. Rates for "renting" 30 seconds of primetime air on network TV during the 2005-2006 viewing season ranged from $293,000 to $705,000 for ten of the most popular shows[7]. And if a company had really deep pockets and wanted to advertise during the NFL's highly rated 2005 Super Bowl, it had to shell out some $2.4 million for just one of those coveted 30-second spots.[8]

Advertising can also be cleverly dressed up and disguised as informational programming. Turn on the TV any time of day and you'll likely see any number of these so-called infomercials touting everything from get-rich real estate courses to age-defying skin care to dramatic weight loss programs to the ever-popular "set-it-and-forget-it" rotisserie oven. You don't have to watch long to see ordinary people claiming their lives have been amazingly transformed or made increasingly better after ordering and using these products. Whether it's paid actors or actual customers, they gush with superlatives about how great the product is, rave enthusiastically about how they made millions after being so close to bankruptcy, or gleefully express how they lost pound after pound on such and such diet.

Now, just imagine if you could harness that same kind of unabashed excitement and exhilarating joy and share it with others when you're advertising God. You don't need a big stage like TV, just a faithful heart and an obedient desire to do God's will whenever and wherever you can (and it never hurts to borrow some of the enthusiasm of the infomercial huckster either!). Your excitement and passion for Christ is definitely contagious and helps excite those who see and hear your message to the point that hopefully they're convinced to go out and get God for themselves or perhaps reaffirm their commitment to serving and worshiping Him.

It should be an easy sell for you. After all, God pitches the best thing going and He does everything those TV products do and then some. God changes your life for the better. God creates a wealth of life-changing opportunities by setting you free from the debt of sin. God helps you lose the weight of excess worry and stress. God is therapeutic and can cure every disease and ailment known to man in less time than it takes you to read this sentence. God cooks up heavenly food for thought and divine little nuggets you can really sink your teeth into for spiritual nourishment. And, like some of those "as seen on TV" products, God gives you an extra bonus when you act on His offer—the gift of life eternal with God in heaven. Now that's an offer you, and all who see and hear you advertising God, just can't resist!

## It's All in the Message

It's the advertiser's job to influence. It's up to you how you receive and process the message. Christians face a similar challenge when advertising God. There will always be people who are more receptive to God's message than others. Those who recognize and accept that they have a strong need to invite Christ into their lives are the easiest ones to sell on God's infinite goodness. In marketing terms, these people are called "prospects" because they represent the ones most likely to act on the message. Because the majority of us like to take the path of least resistance, we tend to gravitate towards those folks first since they require minimal effort and need less convincing to "buy" into God's grace and goodness. The type of people in this group have a strong desire to come to Christ or get more involved in the church, and they are just waiting for that one invitation or gentle and persistent nudge from you to do just that.

Christians who love and serve the Lord should want to invite others to experience the same kind of joy and fellowship with Christ that they have. But it's surprising just how many churchgoers don't actually do this. It reminds me of the new kid at school who sits quietly in the grass at recess with his head cupped in his hands watching all the other kids play and have fun. He wants to play very badly, but won't take the initiative to join in on his own. He wants the others to invite him into the group as a sign of acceptance. It's the same with the unchurched. Many people really do want to be invited to church because it gives them a sense of being wanted and welcomed. Why do you think "you never asked," is a typical response to the question "how come you never…?" A simple invitation is sometimes all it takes to bring someone one step closer to Christ.

On the other hand, people who don't think they need God are a much tougher group to win over. It's quite likely persons in this group believe in God and maybe even go so far as to acknowledge Jesus Christ as the Messiah and Savior. They're just not sold on the fact that Jesus is *their* personal Lord and Savior or that they need Him as the guiding force in their life. Christians advertising God have to invest more time, energy and patience in order to close the sale with these guys. Because people in this don't-need-God group have heard the same messages time and time again over the years, they've probably developed some semblance of immunity and aversion to anything you say and do. Their view from the pew is that it's just all the same ol', same ol' they've heard many times before. Blah, blah, blah, the words simply go in one ear and out the other. In other words, you may not be telling them anything they haven't heard hundreds of times before.

Reaching these kinds of people is a real challenge, no doubt about it, and requires you to think a bit more creatively with words and phrases that present God and his exceptional love and goodness in a fresh new way. Corporate advertisers do this all the time by replacing an existing slogan or catchy jingle with another in order to generate new interest in their product. When advertising God, the idea is not to cut and run when you meet resistance. Instead, you have to communicate that we are all seekers of God's love and truth. That none of us is perfect. That we all struggle to live out and fulfill His commands. That all of us experience failures, disappointments and anger. That we're all trying to live a more righteous and purposeful life. Find the one thing you think they can grab hold of, and then tailor your message accordingly.

People who feel disenfranchised from God don't want to feel like they're being preached to, so any type of holier than thou approach is never going to play very well with them. In fact, taking that kind of attitude will likely have an adverse effect and drive them even further away from God and the church. What they need from you is compassionate encouragement to give God another chance. They need patience and understanding, not judging or condemnation.

The United Methodist Church boasts a positioning statement that reads, "Open hearts. Open minds. Open doors." I like that slogan because it suggests the church is open and receptive to *all* people from *all* walks of life. Amazingly, some people don't like the slogan for that very same reason. It bugs them to no end that people they feel "don't fit in" come to their church. Or maybe they say it's okay to welcome all types as long as they don't come to my church. But, the church isn't ours to decide who is welcome and who is not. It is God's house and God's house is open to everyone, not just the ones we deem worthy enough to invite inside. Plus, none of us come to Christ or to worship with a completely pure mind and clean heart. If that were the case, the pews would be empty every single week. Don't alienate potential Christian believers by making them feel like Christ is a magnet for saints instead of a savior for sinners.

Many churches, like my own, that adopt this "open minds, open hearts" philosophy are successfully able to attract people who don't normally attend church to come there by offering personal enrichment classes, recreational activities and sponsoring support groups that don't revolve around traditional church themes. The thinking is that if these unchurched persons get involved on some periphery level at the church, even if it's not overtly Christian in nature, that that involvement will eventually expose them to Christ, lead them to learn more about Him and His message, and encourage them to become an active church member. It's all about getting them in the door and letting you and Christ take it from there.

## Advertise Like the Pros

Advertisers are very good at the art of persuasion so it doesn't hurt to borrow some of the same advertising methodologies used so effectively in the corporate world. Here are some tried-and-true phrases advertising pros frequently employ in order to influence your buying decisions:

**THEY APPEAL TO YOUR VANITY.** Look 10 years younger! Lose 10 pounds in 3 days! Dress like a winner! Be like Mike. You deserve a break today. Because you're worth it. Kills the germs that cause bad breath.

**THEY APPEAL TO YOUR SENSE OF FEAR.** Heart disease is the #1 killer of men ages 40-60. Homes without a security system are an easy target for burglars. Don't be stranded with a flat tire.

**THEY TAP INTO YOUR GREED.** Make $500 with only 30 minutes work! Turn your finances around in 30 days! Grow your portfolio by 25%! Maximize your earnings potential! Make $2000 a week working at home.

**THEY SELL SOLUTIONS.** No more thinning hair. Unclog drains in minutes. Takes grease out of your way. Get virtually spotless dishes. Sit without pain.

**THEY HIT UPON YOUR ASPIRATIONS.** Stuck in a dead-end career? Want a better paying job? Get on the fast track to financial freedom. Your dream home awaits—no money down! Drive home in that new car today!

**THEY PREY ON YOUR EMOTIONS OR SHAME.** Tired of being overweight? Can't pay your bills? Embarrassed by acne? Turned down by another mortgage company?

You've seen that it sometimes takes a little extra creativity to reach an audience that's not quite ready to relinquish their lives to God. Just for fun, let's borrow a page from the advertiser's handbook and see how these same strategies can be effectively used to advertise God to persons stubbornly clinging to an unsaved lifestyle or who don't see the benefits of having a personal relationship with Jesus Christ.

**APPEAL TO THEIR VANITY.** Everyone wants to look and feel their best. Forget all those fancy creams, spa wraps and cosmetic surgeries. If you want to feel better about yourself, create a new you in Christ. Let Him remove the stress and crushing burdens that cause you to eat and drink more and sleep and smile less. Let Him cleanse away the sin that poisons your mind and body.

**APPEAL TO THEIR SENSE OF FEAR.** Fear is a powerful motivator, and when employed correctly, it can help maneuver someone from the ranks of the unsaved into a lifelong relationship with Christ. Get down to the nitty gritty. Find out specific fears and apprehensions someone has about God, address their concerns in your message, and then offer Scripture-based solutions that help abate their fear.

**TAP INTO THEIR GREED.** Money may make the world go around, but it can make one's spiritual life come to a screeching halt when checking accounts, stock portfolios and material possessions become more important than God. Get them to think about storing up riches in heaven, going to work for Christ, discovering the wealth of opportunities in God's mission work and earning a healthy return on spiritual endeavors.

**SELL SOLUTIONS.** Sometimes people know the problem, but not the solution. My grandmother used to say people like this couldn't see the forest through the trees. But as the Christian on the outside looking in, you can use your unique God-focused perspective to help them find answers and achieve positive results. Encourage and give hope with positive statements that affirm God as master problem solver.

**TARGET THEIR ASPIRATIONS.** Everyone has dreams and goals for themselves and their family. Tap into the things people aspire to with empowering phrases such as: Let Christ's love show you how to become a better parent. Put your spiritual talent to work and make God proud of you. Become a better person by reading, studying and applying the Bible every day.

**"PRAY" ON THEIR EMOTIONS.** Emotion can do one of two things. It can either stifle or stimulant change. People who don't know Christ may not know it or won't admit it, but they can never be truly happy and fulfilled without the presence of Christ in their life. Only when they enter into that personal relationship with Jesus will they see how good life can really be as they experience amazing transformation, peace and contentment. So how do you convince them of the truth? Galvanize their emotions by showing them the unhappiness of living a shallow, unfulfilled life or how to break free from the bondage of an addiction.

As Christian servants, we are advertisers of God's loving grace and should be actively engaged in the job of selling God. I'm not suggesting you gather up all your spare cash, produce a TV or radio spot, or roll out a slick print and billboard campaign. Advertising God is often times very subtle like delivering a hot meal to an elderly person, doing yard work for someone in the hospital, chaperoning the youth choir, or donating airplane mileage so others can travel and do mission work abroad. Jesus Christ himself set that example. The big, amazing miracles He performed definitely ramped up the "wow" factor, but they were but a small part of His overall ministry. Many times in the New Testament Gospels, it was Jesus' smallest gestures, actions and words that left indelible, life-changing impressions on people and caused them to seek and follow Him. It can be that way with you too as you use the most basic expressions and deeds to glorify God and minister to others.

## Word of Mouth Pays Off

Advertisers and their creative teams are very good at what they do, but for all of their clever slogans, glamorous imagery and slick sales gimmicks, one of the oldest and still most effective forms of advertising remains word of mouth. Proven beneficial in any business' advertising arsenal, word of mouth is the classic chain reaction that involves you telling a friend, who tells a friend, who in turn then tells another and so on. Inventor and salesman extraordinaire Ron Popiel extols the virtues of word of mouth advertising when selling his rotisserie oven. On his TV infomercials, he claims there are three ways to advertise his product—television, telephone and tell a friend.

Companies big and small rely on positive word of mouth from clients, customers and reviewers to grow their business. Think how many times a friend, loved one or acquaintance has asked if you've ever used such and such product, eaten at so and so restaurant, bought a car from this or that dealership, or asked for a recommendation on the guy who painted your house. You get peace of mind because you have a reasonable assumption of what to expect when you offer up your own patronage. You safely assume, as the company or contractor certainly expects, that if your friend, loved one or acquaintance had good results doing business there, then so will you.

It should come as no surprise then that word of mouth advertising is often extremely lucrative for businesses. That's why a car salesman offers you $100 if your friend buys a car from him, a leasing agent credits your account if someone you know rents an apartment in the same complex, and why companies prominently display customer testimonials in its ads. Word gets around. And business owners and managers realize people are far more likely to purchase from a place that a friend or acquaintance has recommended as opposed to you thumbing blindly through the phone directory and taking a chance on an unknown entity.

## A Committed Christian Pledges to Advertise God in Any Situation

Similarly, God calls every Christian to do word of mouth advertising for Him. Many of you remember the popular TV ads for the E.F. Hutton brokerage company some years back. The announcer always closed each ad with the slogan, "When E.F. Hutton speaks, people listen."

In a perfect world, the same thing would happen when you advertise God—people would stop everything and listen. But, a perfect world ours is not and some people will always turn a blind eye and a deaf ear to anything you say and do in the name of the Lord.

The same kind of thing went on in Jesus' day, too. Many who heard Jesus preach and saw the miracles He performed continued to reject Him and His message time and time again. It's no different now. Regardless of what some people see and hear about God throughout their lifetime, they will stubbornly refuse to accept the truth about Jesus Christ. It's a sad reality of the world we live in. I'm not trying to discourage you because God calls Christians to spread the good news of Jesus Christ to those who don't believe whether you think they'll accept it or not. There are dozens of people you come into contact with every day that you as one individual can have tremendous Christian impact on simply by expressing your love for Christ either vocally or through a simple act of service. Your words or actions can linger in someone's mind and help stimulate positive change in their life.

I know from personal experience that it isn't always easy to speak or stand up for Christ, but I believe it can be made easier when you make a sincere effort to devote your life to Him and allow God to fully occupy your mind and heart. Only when your own personal needs and desires become secondary can you really start putting God first and reacting to what He wants for you. Once you do this, I believe saying and doing wonderful things about and for God can and will become second nature to any Christian believer.

To help get you started, just think of everything God does for you. He loves you unconditionally. He gives you the certainty of eternal life through the sacrifice of Jesus Christ. He provides you with everything you need. He has the power to heal. He promises to be with you at all times through the Holy Spirit. Remember all the positives associated with Jesus and don't be afraid to show and share your love of Christ.

## Give a First Hand Account

A testimonial is an effective way for advertisers to promote their products. Testimonials serve as an honest, first hand account of a person's actual experience with a business or service, and when done correctly, can be a very effective advertising tool. Many companies sprinkle brief testimonials throughout their direct mail or collateral materials, in their catalog and on their web pages to reinforce the quality of their product, the knowledge and friendliness of their sales staff and the timely manner in which they ship items. The thinking is you are far more likely to believe the claims a company makes if an average customer like yourself echoes the satisfaction they experienced.

Likewise, giving a first hand account of your relationship with Jesus Christ is a very powerful tool when advertising God. It's your own personal story, your unique perspective on what Jesus Christ means to you and how He has affected your life. There's no right or wrong way to tell your story and you may not ever tell it quite the same way twice. What makes your testimony so real, so powerful and so moving to others is the honesty, emotion and heartfelt conviction of your words and your story.

To deliver a strong and energetic testimony, you don't have to be a one-armed athlete, a bad celebrity gone good or someone who has overcome a hard knock life. Normal everyday "joes" can get in on the action of advertising God, too. We all have our own compelling stories to tell, so don't underestimate the power of yours and its ability to inspire and affect others.

You know where you were before you met Christ and where you are now in Christ. And because the journey has different highs and lows for all, yours is a one-of-a-kind tale that never grows old, never grows boring. In fact, I strongly believe that testimony from ordinary people like you and I can be much more dramatic and influential than that delivered by famous speakers. I'm not questioning the honesty or validity of their testimony. I just think others may very well identify with you and your situation much easier than they ever could a Hollywood star, some sports hero or a rags-to-riches media darling.

Based on their status and name recognition, celebrities will always draw much larger crowds than all of us no-names. But advertising God isn't always about speaking to thousands in sold-out arenas across the world, which can be distant and impersonal. Most of the time, sharing a heartfelt and emotional first hand account of God's divine love and goodness happens in the coziness of one on one or in small groups. The next time you feel the need to share your personal story, remember that you don't need a huge crowd to endorse God, just an audience of one.

## God is for Me, So Why Do I Feel Everyone's Against Me?

Re-read Ephesians 5:1—you are charged with being an imitator of God. Instead of shrinking back in silence, know that God has called *you* to be *His* witness to all the world. If you're still struggling with word of mouth advertising and sharing your faith, it's time to redirect your focus. Rather than feeling burdened by the call to advertise God, accept the opportunity joyfully knowing that God—almighty God in heaven!—has singled you out to be an important contributor to His kingdom. You are definitely a most valuable addition to God's evangelical team.

Think of it this way. God knows you by name and has chosen you to be His personal ambassador and servant. God knows your situation, your time constraints and your weaknesses, but He still has called YOU. Is there really any greater honor in life than to hear and answer God's call? Most of you would jump at a service opportunity if the Governor of your state or President of the United States called. How much greater, then, is a spiritual summons from God? If God believes in you, you should have the faith and courage to believe in yourself and in the message you were born to share. Open your heart and your hands. Make your voice heard and your actions seen in the name of Jesus Christ. Let someone know you are a Christian today by what you say, what you do and what you stand for. Don't do it for your own pride or to boost your own ego, but do it solely and expressly for God's honor and glory. In other words, don't let allow yourself as the messenger to become more important than the message.

There are always going to be those who are aligned against you, but know this. They cannot prevent you from carrying out God's message and plan if God desires that His message and plan be carried out. Pharaoh tried to stop Moses by slaughtering innocent boy babies, but failed. Saul and Goliath tried to stop David from becoming the great king of Israel, but failed. The Jewish leaders tried to keep Jesus in the tomb, but failed. Emperors tried to prevent the spread of the early Christian church, but failed. People may put obstacles and impediments in your way, but when God sends you out, they will fail to stop His work as well. Take heart in what Paul writes in Romans 8:31, "If God is for us, who can be against us?"

## UP FOR DISCUSSION.

1.  People fall into three distinct groups—ones who earnestly want to accept Christ, ones who know about Christ but aren't ready to accept Him, and ones who just tune Him out. Name some ways you can creatively minister to each group.

2.  How do people interpret your "word of mouth" about God? Is it positive or negative?

3.  How does being singled out by God make you feel?

4.  Everyone has a story to tell. Would you consider sharing your salvation story with your Sunday School class, Bible study group or others who could benefit by hearing it?

# 5

## *Spiritual Gifts and Advertising God*

"Each one should use whatever gift he has received to serve others…"

—*{ 1 Peter 4:10 }*

The advertisements you see on TV, hear on the radio, or read in your favorite magazine or newspaper are the end result of months of planning, researching, revising and production work. Millions of dollars in sales and potential profits hinge on single ads or campaigns. Few products are ever successfully advertised on a whim or at the eleventh hour. The monetary stakes involved in creating, producing and placing an ad are simply too great to leave anything to random chance. After a target market is identified and defined, every detail, every image and every word in an ad is carefully strategized, evaluated and calculated in such a way that best influences the company's target consumer to purchase that particular product or service. A well thought out plan is required to ensure success.

But before a company can even think about advertising, they must find the most efficient way to deliver their message to the audience. A company may well produce the greatest ad known to humankind, but if it falls on the wrong ears or isn't seen by the intended target market, the ad is destined to fail. That's why you never see beer commercials during soap operas or ads for ladies' skin care advertised during a college or professional football game. The target audience for those products is simply not there, and the message is lost on people who will likely tune out the message rather than respond to it.

As an agent of God, you too must learn how effectively deliver your testimony or faith message to your intended audience in order to achieve the best possible results. Although much less complicated and laborious than the strategies and principles involved with corporate advertising, there are logical steps you should take in order to maximize your effectiveness when advertising God.

## Discover God's Plan for You

"Before I formed you in the womb I knew you, before you were born I set you apart." If you've never read this verse from Jeremiah 1:5, it's a real eye-opener, isn't it? It confirms you have genuine worth and value in God's kingdom. It tells you that God has a specific plan and purpose for you, even before you are born. In God's eyes, everyone has a reason for being.

Want more proof that you are uniquely special to God? Read Galatians 1:15. Paul says God claimed him from birth. Or recall Isaiah 49:1 where the prophet proclaims, "Before I was born the Lord called me; from my birth He has made mention of my name."

These three verses make it abundantly clear that you too have been identified and claimed by God from birth as well. God has singled you out to do awesome things in the name of the Lord. You just have to grab hold of His love and power and trust God to lead you to do the things He wants you to do.

When I'm writing product copy for a retail catalog, one of the descriptors that customers react favorably to is "one-of-a-kind" because it suggests uniqueness and rarity. God's plan for you is like that. Your plan is personal, a true one-of-a-kind, and no two plans are ever exactly the same. Regardless of how you were conceived, where you were born, or who your parents are, God created you and I for a specific reason. Believing otherwise is a tactic Satan uses to discourage, deceive and ultimately defeat you by eroding your confidence and resolve to do the work God intended. So don't go there! I can't say it enough—no one is a mistake or insignificant in God's eyes and your life is important to God.

Although God has a plan for every one of us, it's up to each individual to seek and live out that plan. From the youngest to the oldest, weakest to the strongest, wealthiest to the poorest, God gives people of all ages and abilities unique talents they can use to do great and mighty works in the name of Jesus Christ. It's not just the big, obvious talents like teaching, praying or healing, either. It's also gifts like compassion, empathy, giving, listening and wisdom that can be put into service for God. Look around, and you'll find plenty of ordinary people just like you who have willingly picked up their cross, fully embraced their talent, and are now sharing the good news of Jesus Christ wherever and whenever they can in all sorts of creative and exciting ways. There's no reason you can't do the same. Take charge of the plan God lays out before you and become one of those who joyfully advertise God wherever that may be.

Some people are fortunate enough to discover and get actively involved in their purpose early in life, while others struggle to find their place, even well into their adult years. If you're one who is patiently and prayerfully waiting for God to reveal His plan for you, remain watchful, attentive and hopeful. It may not come in the loud and obvious ways you expect. In 1 Kings 19:11-13, Elijah was told by an angel to stand on the mountain and wait for God to pass by. A violent wind came, then an earthquake, then a fire, but God was not in any of these events. Rather, the presence of God came to Elijah in a gentle whisper.

It may very well be in a whisper when God reveals His plans to you as well. Maybe it starts when you get inspired after hearing a sermon, reading an article or seeing something on TV. What begins as a small, and seemingly unimportant event, could signal the recognition of your plan or become the catalyst that sends you off on your life's calling. Our God is a truly awesome God, but that doesn't mean He always communicates with us in loud and obvious ways. Stubbornly insist on waiting around for that thunderclap, lightning bolt or some other demonstrative event and you might miss God's whisper altogether.

In order to discover God's ultimate plan for you, you have to tune out anything that hinders your relationship with God. Pray relentlessly for God's loving guidance to direct you to where you need to go. Practice the patience we talked about. And pay attention. You'll find that God does indeed speak to you in so many unique ways—through worship, prayer and Bible study, the advice of a friend, the persistence of your minister, the voice of a child, a cry for help. The ways God communicates with us are too numerous to list. However you discover it, once your hear and identify God's plan for you, go out and put it to good use for the glory of His kingdom.

## Wait for the Lord

God is the wondrous architect of life who can build and shape you into a dynamic Christian voice and energetic servant if you just open yourself to His presence and respond to His call. Learning to sincerely and humbly defer to God draws you nearer to Him and puts you closer to discovering and invoking your true purpose.

That's not always the easiest thing to do. Especially when, as you seek out God's plan, the things you want to do and the things God wants you to do are in conflict instead of harmony. Finding fulfillment in the life God promises you is tough because we live in a society that thrives on instant gratification. Attention spans are fleeting, so the quicker things are, the better. We like fast food, speedy checkout lines, microwave ovens, high-speed Internet connections, HOV lanes, instant messaging and on-demand movies. Waiting around is not something we're conditioned to do very well. If something doesn't offer instant appeal, we move on. No wonder it's difficult for so many to hear and wait on God. He may not always move at the breakneck speed we like.

If you're struggling to discover God's plan, chances are you're going to grow impatient or frustrated. And when you do, it's mighty tempting to race full throttle past God down the road of life, shifting your own desires and goals ahead of His. Some may find the self-gratification they're after, but the Christian who patiently waits for God knows temporary satisfaction apart from God never translates into long-term happiness. That's because you end up living for yourself and not following the more purposeful path God has mapped out for you. It's like the child who thumbs her nose at the wise parent, then goes off and makes mistake after mistake rather than heeding the advice of one who has been there before and knows a better way.

Whenever you stop seeking the counsel of God and lose the humble patience that allows Him to be your guide, you're absolutely putting yourself first and God second. Your ego and your willingness to submit to God are suddenly at spiritual odds with one another. God wants you to do this; you want to do that. Maybe you pray about it and feel conflicted because your head says God is moving you in one direction while your heart directs you in another. But some people don't or won't even take the time to pray about it or seek spiritual advice. They stubbornly think they have it all figured out and leap forward doing whatever it is they think is best without waiting on God.

Even worse, some Christians keep Jesus at arm's length, reaching for Him only when they feel like they really, really need Him to solve a problem, heal a disease, mend a relationship, or intervene in a crisis. For these people, Jesus is a last resort, not the premier influence in their life. And that's a shame, because we serve and worship a wondrous, magnificent God full of abundant love, grace and forgiveness.

It's exactly this kind of arrogance and impatience that Satan loves to exploit. He loves messing with your mind and trying to convince you that you know yourself better than God knows you, that your way is better, that you don't really need Him, or that it's your life and you should be in charge of your own destiny. If you feel tempted to sprint out ahead of God, remember that, like the good shepherd or wise parent, God knows what's best for you. It's not that He wants to hold you back or deprive you of any good thing. It's just that He knows what you need and the best avenue for you to pursue. You can't claim to put God first when you dash out in front of Him, then look back to see what it is He wants you to do.

Think about Peter when he saw Jesus walking on the water. With his eyes focused squarely on Jesus, Peter, so bold and confident, stepped out of the boat and began walking on the water to meet the Lord. As the winds howled and the stormy sea crashed against his body, Peter panicked. He took his eyes off Christ and focused his attention instead on the danger and turmoil splashing about him. Only then did the sea's angry waves and watery grasp began to pull Peter down further and further, threatening to drown him. Terrified, Peter cried out to the Lord, and being only an arm's length away, Jesus reached out and lifted him up from the tumultuous water.

Perhaps that famous Biblical scene is a metaphor for those who rush out ahead of Christ vainly searching for God's plan and rarely, if at all, take the time to look back. Because Jesus is behind them, they lose sight of Him. And because their eyes are no longer trained on Christ, they can't possibly devote their full attention to Him. They're looking squarely down the path ahead and at all the obstacles blocking the way. Like Peter, since they're not focused on Christ, they rapidly begin to sink into temptation, into fear, into doubt, into denial, into unhappiness, into sin. And, if they're unable to cut free and swim up to breathe in the life-sustaining mercy and redemption of Jesus Christ, they drown in an unfulfilled, unpurposed life.

The good news is that it's never too late to turn around and wait for Christ to catch up. Just like He was there when Peter was sinking into the sea, Jesus is always near, ready to extend a loving hand when you cry out. If you've dashed ahead of Christ in search of God's direction, turn around, admit your mistake to God and ask for forgiveness. Let Jesus raise you up from whatever abyss threatens you and restore you to safe ground. Only then can you really discover the purposeful calling God has in store for you.

If you need extra encouragement to discourage you from jumping out ahead of God, read and apply the message from Psalm 27:14, "Wait for the Lord; be strong and take heart and wait for the Lord." In general, we humans are a pretty impatient group, so waiting on God is sometimes difficult. But be patient. God's plan for you will be revealed on His terms, not yours. Take heart in His promises, keep your eyes squarely on Christ and pray diligently and faithfully for guidance and revelation.

## Recognize and Embrace Your Talent

All of us have unique gifts we can use to further God's work, and God's plan for you likely calls for you to use such gifts. For some Christians, the spiritual gifts they possess are easy to discern, and these people are in a ministry or position that puts their talents and strengths to best use. Others, however, find identifying their spiritual gifts isn't so easy. Out of frustration or discouragement, they may even convince themselves that they have no viable gifts to use for God, and in the time they waste convincing themselves this Satan-generated falsehood to be true, they squander away valuable spiritual gifts and unique talents through stubbornness, pride and procrastination. The truth is, it can take many hours of introspection, heartfelt prayer and counseling with a pastor or spiritual leader before you come to recognize and accept your spiritual gifts. And, frankly, that's time some Christians just aren't willing to invest. As a result, they never ripen into the fruitful, productive servants Jesus calls them to be.

Of course, identifying your spiritual gifts is only half the process. You must passionately embrace your gifts and put them to work for the betterment of God's kingdom. In James 2:17, the Bible teaches faith without action is dead. What good is it for us to spend time narrowing down and honing our spiritual gifts, then never using them? It's like going to college, assimilating years of knowledge and earning a degree, then never pursuing a career or business opportunities in your field.

Like the degree that just sits there gathering dust, your spiritual gifts can lay dormant, too, if not put to good use. Those who shelve their spiritual gifts become the seed that falls among the thorns in Jesus' parable of the four soils in Matthew 13:1-23. They hear and accept the Word, but the routines and difficulties of daily life, coupled with the material pursuits of worldly happiness, combine to choke the Word and render these individuals unfocused and unproductive.

If you're one who continues to engage in this kind of passive action while ignoring your spiritual gifts, you really have to wonder how long it will be before God moves on to someone else who will do the "something" He really wants you to do. Instead of you being blessed, it will be another who gets the honor and privilege of cheerfully and obediently seizing the moment and shining for God.

Don't let that happen. Harness the power of your spiritual gifts and make yourself available to God so you can stop making excuses and start putting your faith into action. Not so that God doesn't have to use someone else, but because God has blessed you with a specific gift that He wants you to use to glorify and grow His kingdom. Think of how worse off the world would be if Billy Graham ignored his call to evangelism, or Mother Teresa decided not to follow her passion to help the poor, or C.S. Lewis blew off his gift of the written word.

Like all these great believers, you too are uniquely talented and have something very special to offer God. If you go through life ignoring your talent or gift, it's going to be a real setback to growing the community of Christ. All the great and mighty things you and you alone could have accomplished in the name of Christ are forever lost simply because you chose to ignore your spiritual gift. I always wonder how many great musicians, artists, writers, teachers, doctors and so on are out there, but no one knows about their talent because they choose not to use it.

As you grow in your faith, lay claim to your spiritual gift and begin to seek out service opportunities, never assume God cannot use you to advertise and promote His message. Regardless of your age, income, social status, faith background or what society may tell you, you have unique abilities and innate talents that make you worthy of receiving God's love and entering into productive discipleship for Him. Did you get that? Everyone has a talent they can use to advertise God. Yes, that means YOU! Now substitute some words to make it your own personal affirmation.

I have a talent or skill I can use to advertise God!

Write that sentence down. Carry it in your wallet. Attach it to your bathroom mirror. Tape it on your desk or computer monitor. If it seems like I'm making a big deal out of this affirmation I am! You'd be surprised how many Christians feel shortchanged in the talent department and simply give up before they ever try to advertise God. I don't want you to be one of those people.

Think back to Paul's message in Galatians 1:15. Like Paul, you have been set apart from birth. You've got something worthy and valuable to offer God, so use whatever talent you've got to the very best of your ability to glorify Him.

And when I use the word talent, I'm not talking exclusively about a performance talent such as singing, playing a musical instrument, dancing or acting. Talent is a skill, a passion or a natural ability gifted to you by our oh-so generous God that you can use in some way, shape or form to do His work. Take a look at Romans 12:6-8 and 1 Corinthians 12:4-11 and you'll see talent can be everything from listening to healing, serving to leading, teaching to giving. And don't think the gifts listed there are the only ones God offers us. There are so many more!

Because all of us are unique individuals with our own special talents, you won't always have the same spiritual gifts as everyone else. In fact, your spiritual gift may not be all that common or even listed in the Bible. And that's okay provided it is God-centered and Biblically sound. Everyone's talent is different. Which is exactly the way God intended it to be. I think it's His unique way of helping the legions of Christian believers maximize their potential for doing marvelous and wonderful things achieved in God's name.

Like I said, identifying your spiritual gift isn't always as easy as it seems. I know it can be confusing and frustrating. Most church leaders have a quick "test" you can take that will help you recognize and narrow down your specific talent. These tests vary widely in scope from one denomination to another, but if you're having a hard time pinpointing your exact gifts, I urge you to meet with your pastor or worship leader for advice or to take such a test. If you're more of a do-it-yourselfer, go online to Google or Yahoo, type in "spiritual gifts + tests" and you'll find plenty of links there as well. Once you discover what your talent is, don't just let it sit there and wither. Find at least one way you can use that talent of yours to glorify Jesus Christ every single day.

*Advertising God in Real Life:*

*Dana is diagnosed with breast cancer and after undergoing chemotherapy loses her hair. Like other patients receiving treatment in the radiation unit, Dana hates the thought of wearing some hokey-looking wig and all the hats friends bring by just look silly.*

*One day, Dana grabs one of her son's buffs that he wears under his football helmet and, without paying it any attention, quickly ties it around her head before heading off to treatment. One of the other cancer patients there that day comments on how positive and uplifting the words are printed on Dana's buff. Unaware of the message, Dana asks what the buff says. Work hard, fight hard, seize the victory, the woman reads. She asks Dana where she can get one and says she knows other patients who would love having one, too.*

*Dana thinks about the woman's words. Even in the midst of her illness, Dana feels like God is giving her a unique opportunity to make a difference. As one who has a skill and passion for making her own clothes, Dana prays for clarity and direction and feels God encouraging her. Dana enlists the supportive and enthusiastic help of her best friend Monica, and the next day the two women buy materials and secure the pro bono services of a local screenprinter.*

*A few weeks later, Dana is passing out free buffs to all the cancer patients who want one at the radiology area. Dana tells them it is a way to keep God's love and healing power on their minds at every phase of their treatment. The message reads Believe In Christ, Believe In Yourself.*

*The buffs prove to be immensely popular and when demand rapidly increases, dozens of women in Dana's church volunteer to sew as many buffs as needed so no woman who wants one will have to go without. Word about Dana's ministry begins to get around and her idea quickly spreads to other cities across the state and country.*

*Dana advertises God by using her talent and her cancer situation to help others find profound courage and hope in the healing power of Jesus Christ.*

## Put Your Spiritual Gifts to Good Use

By now, I hope I've convinced you that you are indeed one of God's most valuable servants and have a special talent worth sharing. Now you need to determine how best to use your talent and put it to good use. The best way to do this is to spend meaningful time with God in prayer. The Bible tells us that, as was His custom, Jesus prayed every time He was confronting a task or preparing to perform a miracle. When you pray, ask God to give you that same kind of courage and conviction to pursue whatever opportunity or challenge He puts before you and start listening for God's whispers! Move forward confidently knowing you have the distinct honor and privilege of doing the work Christ has called you to do.

For those who are still actively and prayerfully seeking out their true God purpose, however, continue to pray about it and be patient. Remember, God's plan isn't always revealed in a burning bush or thunderous boom. All of us would love it if God called on the phone or sent an e-mail detailing exactly when and how He wants us to use our spiritual gifts. But that wouldn't require any type of faith commitment on our part.

The reality is, God does tell us what He wants us to do and when—we just have to learn how to react and respond to the opportunities He gives us instead of second-guessing and over-thinking everything. Because God is an active participant in our lives, I believe He talks to us a lot. Unfortunately, we don't always tune in or trust what He is saying. We may even be confused about the direction in which He's nudging us, especially if it's not something we expect or have planned for. If you feel God is speaking to what He wants you to do and where He wants you to go, but feel you're unable to discern or understand His message, again, consult with your minister, a Christian friend mature in their faith or a trusted lay person for clarity.

Learning to humbly accept God's guidance is the first step towards recognizing and empowering your passion and purpose. Stay faithful and find encouragement in God's promise that He has laid claim to you, then pledge to always love, honor and obey God in all things and trust Him to help you fulfill the purpose for which you have been set apart from birth.

## Even the Weakest Can Become More Christ-Like

Because God blesses all of us with unique talents and gifts, I find it extremely bothersome that many Christians make illogical assumptions and arrogant declarations about who can and cannot take on certain roles and responsibilities in God's kingdom work. As sinful human creatures, we all have shortcomings that we struggle with every day. But thankfully, God can and will help you overcome your weaknesses so you can discover your individual talents and capitalize on them as well. The arms of Christ open wide enough to embrace everyone. Think about stuttering Moses who tried to convince God he wasn't the best one to demand Pharaoh set the Israelites free. Or a drunken Noah who embarrassed himself in front of his sons. David wrote so many of the impassioned and beloved Psalms, but selfishly committed adultery with Uriah's wife Bathsheba, then callously had Uriah murdered so David could take Bathsheba as his own spouse. Consider Matthew, despised by the people for being a tax collector. Or Peter who adamantly promised to follow Christ to the death, but later denied Him three times when confronted with the threat of eminent danger to his own life. And then there's Paul, history's greatest apostle, yet he was once an impassioned zealot so bent on destroying the early church that he actively tortured and persecuted thousands of Christians.

All these great persons of faith had their fair share of weaknesses, yet God used them in unique and memorable ways. Perhaps the Bible mentions their weaknesses as encouragement to all of us and as a loving reminder that we don't have to be saints in order to be effective agents and servants of Jesus Christ. According to Hebrews 4:15, Jesus sympathizes with our weaknesses because He experienced the same weaknesses himself, yet still He did the Father's will. Don't let your weakness choke your desire and resolve to advertise God. Overcome your inadequacies by confessing them to Christ and seeking His strength.

## Let God Be Your Guide

As we go through the motions of everyday life, it's so easy to get off task from the most important mission of the day—focusing entirely on God's desires instead of our own and sharing His message whenever we can as we go about our daily routine. My wife and I once saw the message "If God is your co-pilot, switch seats" on a church sign near our house. And it's true. We don't need to be sharing the controls with God or flying solo. Having God as our second in command means He is not the one in charge, not the one giving the orders, not the one we're answering or held accountable to.

When it comes to true repentance and overcoming weaknesses, you have to relinquish control and wholly surrender yourself to God. That means lessening your own wants and desires so God can do more. Or think of it this way. The more you stubbornly cling to doing things your way, the less God can do in your life.

It's not easy to let go of your ego and surrender control to God. Plenty of people, including Christians, have priorities and personal desires that benefit them first and God second. If those same priorities and desires just so happen to coincide with priorities and needs that benefit the church or God's kingdom, then so much the better. It's a win-win. But when these same wants and priorities differ, then there's conflict because many people invariably do what they want instead of what God wants.

It's time for Christians to move past this kind of self-centered thinking. After all, do you want to be the kind of person who stores up your treasures on earth or in heaven? Jesus teaches in Matthew 6:33 for us to seek first His kingdom and His righteousness. Everything after that will fall into place. The number one priority any Christian should have is serving our almighty God, not living every day for one's own self.

So how do you move from a self-centered lifestyle to one of humbleness and servitude? I wish I had the magic answer for you here, but it's not that simple. Because we've had years of individual practice rebelling against God, it's unrealistic to expect things will dramatically change overnight. But change can and will come eventually if you really want it to come. It starts by becoming more receptive to God as you pray, worship and study the Bible, and by becoming more tuned in to the plan God has for you. Instead of making excuses and selfishly pursuing your own pleasures and pursuits, give in to God and let Him help you take the focus off yourself so you can redirect your focus more towards Him. Your life is a gift from God and it was never meant to be all about you! Make the defining moments in your life center around God and all the things you do for Him. At the end of life, few Christians look back and fondly recall all the great things they did for themselves. Instead, I believe most of us remember the good works and deeds we did for others by following the example of Christ and serving Him.

Another positive thing you can do to exact change in your life is not getting discouraged when you feel resistance to letting God take charge of things.

Remember, no one is perfect and we all struggle with selfishness to varying degrees. To remedy this mindset, envision your will and God's will as two parallel lines. As you grow and evolve in your faith, your goal should be to position those two lines closer and closer together until they become one, concentrated on a single, spirit-driven purpose and always moving in unison towards the same end point. Let God be the one who guides you, then put your trust in Him. The results may astound you in ways you never even imagined. Instead of being self-centered become more self-sacrificing. Distance yourself from the foolishness and follies of the world and allow the directive and purposeful spirit of Christ to fully take root in you.

Paul tells us in Philippians 4:13 that we can do everything through Him who gives us strength. Pay attention to the wording in that verse. Paul doesn't say *some* things. He says *all* things. I firmly believe that when God calls you to do something, He equips you with everything you need to successfully complete the task. All you need to do is have a little faith in Him. I know many times that walk of faith seems like stepping off a cliff into thin air without strapping on a safety line or parachute. Taking that faith walk may defy all rational thought, but you have to get to the point were you know with absolute certainty that God will be there to prevent you from falling. Sometimes a task seems illogical, impractical or too monumental, but remember, nothing is impossible with God. Thinking otherwise plays right into Satan's hands by minimizing God's greatness. Have this kind of attitude and you risk becoming one who negatively advertises God in front of others by imposing limitations on Him instead of celebrating how awesome His love, grace and majesty really are.

I'm not saying it's easy to take this kind of faith walk because lots of times it is not. Being a servant of Christ carries no promise or guarantee of being easy. And frankly, if it were, your faith would never be tested or strengthened when you blindly followed Christ down whatever path He asks you to take. Sometimes the way is dark, frightful, intimidating and fraught with pitfalls. Even the strongest Christians can grow tired, frustrated and burned out. But even amid your personal struggles, God's love and power are a constant, so take peace and comfort knowing, just as Christ was there with Peter as he walked on stormy waters, so too is He is always there with you to lend a helping hand or lift you back up from all the dangerous seas that threaten to swallow you. I love how prophet Isaiah recognizes this spiritual truism and praises God's empowering strength in Isaiah 40:29-31.

> "He gives strength to the weary
> and increases the power of the weak.
> Even youths grow tired and weary,
> and young men stumble and fall;
> but those who hope in the Lord
> will renew their strength.
> They will soar on wings like eagles;
> they will run and not grow weary,
> they will walk and not be faint."

Jesus tells us that we must deny ourselves when we make the decision to pick up our Cross, embrace God's plan and gifts, and follow Him. That means ridding yourself of every selfish action, every fear and doubt, every misguided loyalty, every single thing that inhibits your relationship with Him. It means putting God first and yourself second, or third, or dead last if the situation warrants. I think Jesus himself expresses the idea best in Luke 9:25 when He asks "What good is it for a man to gain the whole world, and yet lose or forfeit his very self?" We may have mapped out a life plan that feeds on success, status and security, but if we don't have a life in Christ, we really don't have a life at all.

## UP FOR DISCUSSION.

1.  Do you feel like you've discovered God's plan for you? If not, why? What is God's plan for you? What steps are you taking to live out your plan and put it into practice?

2.  How can you better hear and understand what God is saying? How does it benefit you to wait patiently on God instead of rushing out ahead of Him?

3.  What does it say about you and your faith when you put your own wants and needs above those of God? What are some ways you can put God first?

4.  What talent or skill do you have that could be put to use for the glory of God?

5.  If you don't—or won't—use the talent you know you have, how does it make you feel knowing God might simply move on to someone else who will use that same talent to benefit Him?

# 6

# *Faith, Deeds and Advertising God*

o o o o o o o o o o o o o o o o o o o o o o o o o o o o o o o

"Whatever you do, work at it with all your heart…it is the Lord Christ you are serving."

—{ *Colossians 3:23-24* }

In the world of competitive business, companies that thrive and succeed over the long haul are not the ones content to sit still or rest comfortably on their laurels. In a capitalism-based society, a business that is not consistently moving forward ultimately falls behind its competition. It is Darwin's theory of nature applied to a free market society—only the strong survive. Successful companies fill a void in the marketplace by aggressively creating new and improved products and services, and in conjunction with strategic advertising, subsequently generate customer demand for their offerings.

As consumers, it seems like wherever we go we are barraged with advertisements for every product imaginable. That's because advertisers follow the old adage of go where the people are. Ads are seen and heard in our homes, in our workplace, in our cars, in our e-mails, on our cell phones, in our mailboxes, on our DVDs, and tucked inside our credit card bills. It seems almost impossible to escape the marketing reach of these savvy, assertive advertisers.

I think the Christian community ought to adopt the thought process of the aggressive advertiser. In other words, to better target our audience, church leaders and Christians alike must go to where the people are so they can readily see and hear us advertising God. We should be out there earning and upholding the reputation that we, as faithful followers of Christ, will advertise God via whatever channels are available to us. We need to be everywhere the eyes can see and everywhere a Christian voice needs to be heard. We need to be in the places people expect us to be and in the unexpected places they don't. It's about more than throwing money at something. It's about rolling up our sleeves and getting down in the trenches doing God's work and getting the word out about Him wherever that might be.

## You Don't Need Money, Just a Servant's Heart

Collectively with fellow church members and other faith-based groups, we Christians have the talents, energy and resources needed to simultaneously get God's message out to plenty of people in plenty of areas just like the aggressive advertiser. We simply start by advertising Him with real zeal in our established social circles at church, school, work, neighborhood gatherings and family get-togethers, then fan out into the community to become the impassioned advertisers God wants us to be.

My church, for instance, takes an active role in community outreach to show others that we are a Christ-focused congregation whose lives reflect what we believe. Sometimes, such service projects takes on some rather unorthodox types of work. Examples of past efforts include passing out free doughnuts to nurses, police officers and sales clerks working on Christmas Eve, cleaning toilets in busy stores, even pumping gas, cleaning windshields and checking tire pressure for motorists at a corner gas station. At no time did anyone in our group pepper the recipients of the service with Bible verses or aggressively invite them to church. If anyone asked why we were out there doing what we were doing, we simply replied, "God's love is free and so is this gift." Some went a little further and explained we were doing servant evangelism work in the name of Jesus Christ for our church. Most who questioned us were pleasantly surprised by our motives, and some even commented how they wished their own church did community outreach projects like this.

When we're out there doing Christ's work, we hopefully plant a seed in someone's mind to come to church and commit their life to Christ, or if they're already involved in a church, inspire them to get their own church more involved advertising God in the community.

If you're super wealthy and have a strong desire to spend big money on an all-out marketing blitz to advertise God, then more power to you. For the rest of us, however, God banks on us to get out there and advertise Him by word of mouth and by doing the every day things, big and small, that He asks of us.

Most of this daily service work is not glamorous or earth shattering. Instead, it can be very humbling at times, but very rewarding as well. Participating in relief projects, teaching Bible School, taking meals to the elderly and the ill, counseling and praying with those in need, making donations of food and clothing to shelters, even pumping someone's gas or cleaning their toilets—these are the kind of unselfish deeds and actions that demonstrate genuine love and passion for the ministries of Jesus Christ. The kinds of things Christ himself would have done. And while deeds such as these may seem small on the surface, they are not inconsequential because your actions have the potential to make a tangible difference in someone's life. Such faithful deeds say to those on the receiving end of your efforts that the body of Christ is lovingly reaching out to them, that these people are important to you and that you faithfully respond to the teachings and call of Christ no matter how large or how humble the task.

## The Four Commandments of Advertising

For all God has done for us, He asks very little in return, and as John reminds us in 1 John 5:3 "His commands are not burdensome." In return for sending Jesus Christ to save us from death and eternal separation from our Lord, all God requires is that we confess our sins, profess our belief in Him, share His message and teachings with others and live our lives accordingly by putting Christ first in everything we do.

Adopting a Christ-first attitude means you can no longer sit passively by in a world that needs to see, hear and experience the unconditional love and forgiveness God offers. God has a life-changing, life-saving product called salvation that needs to be prolifically advertised to everyone whenever the opportunity arises. Think about it. God's salvation message is the quintessential good news and brings with it great joy and peace. Hebrews 13:8 proclaims that Jesus is precisely the same yesterday, today and forever. God never changes. God's message is not something that's new and improved, updated, or modified in any way to change with the times. Not many products can make that claim!

As believers committed to advertising God, it's our job to deliver this, the greatest of all messages, to God's target audience wherever they may be. In advertising speak, there is a void in the marketplace, and Christians are the ones called to fill that void and that need in whatever ways we can. Not necessarily by advertising on TV or radio, but in more of a grass roots kind of way as we pass along the good news of Jesus Christ from one individual to another without prejudice or condition. God's salvation is offered up for everyone fair and square, and that's what makes God's grace even greater. No one deserves His love and salvation, but He freely gives it to us all, unworthy as we are.

By following the advertising strategies of thriving businesses, you learn effective techniques you can use every day to share God's message. Think of it as advertising 101. There are four essential steps involved in successful advertising—attention, interest, desire and action, or A.I.D.A. as it's referred to in the advertising business. I believe all four of these proven, time-tested principles can be similarly applied when the church and its Christian believers share their witness to others.

## 1. Capture Their Attention

A great ad cuts through the clutter and becomes ingrained in people's minds. A great ad achieves its objective and delivers results. Conversely, you can have the greatest product or ad people have ever seen or heard about, but if no one's interested in what you're saying or selling, you don't have an audience. And if you don't have an audience, you have no one with whom to share your message. Your ad is simply tuned out or gets lumped into the "who cares?" category.

Most ads have only a precious few seconds to catch your attention or create what advertiser's term "the hook." Think of how many ads or products you flip past in magazines and catalogs, or all those commercials you tune out on your TV or car radio. Ads and products that are summarily ignored have one thing in common—they fail to grab your interest or differentiate themselves in any beneficial way from all the others you see and hear. Because the hook isn't there, the message doesn't grab you.

It's the same way with advertising God. Many times, you have only a few seconds to make your voice heard or get God's message across in some meaningful way. I can't say it enough. When an opportunity to advertise God occurs, you have to make the moment count. If you're slow to speak or hesitant to act in this fast-paced world, few people will stop long enough to let you and your message catch up. They will just move on and you lose out on another opportunity to advertise God.

## Competition for Our Attention is Fierce

We are inundated every day with a variety of messages from the time the radio alarm buzzes us awake in the morning until the time we nod off to sleep at night—everything from your spouse reminding you of an errand, to instructions from your boss, to voice mails and text messages, to cell phone calls, to pop-up ads and spam e-mails on your computer. We live in a society obsessed with communication and the sharing of ideas. You can't blame people for simply tuning out. That's precisely why, as Christians advertising God in a message-laden world, we have to give people a compelling reason to listen and pay attention to what we have to say. And not just hear our message, but turn around and promptly act on it.

Unfortunately I can't give you that universal catch phrase or guaranteed one-liner that will always resonate and make people pay attention to you. Because God made us all unique individuals with our own set of special skills and spiritual gifts, no one can be all things to all people. What works for you may not work for me. And what works effectively for you with a particular audience this time may not be as successful on another person or group the next. Advertising God requires evolving and adapting.

I'll give you a real world illustration. When condensing the text of this book into a series of Sunday school lessons I was asked to lead, I knew each week's message content had to be flexible enough to appeal to a variety of different personalities in the group. I knew talkers in the class would enjoy lively and spirited discussion. They wouldn't respond well to a traditional "lecture" style teaching, so the lesson had to include plenty of stimulating questions and less talking by yours truly. Others in the class might be more quiet and reticent, unwilling or unable to share their thoughts and opinions. For them, I had to craft a message that also guided the discussion, gently nudging them to a place where they felt more comfortable opening up. I also had to be aware of topics too critical or too divisive for their age and demographic group so as not to polarize the group.

To capture one's attention in the best way possible, you sometimes have to tailor your message to fit the demographics and mindset of your audience or pull examples from your own life experiences so persons can better relate to what you're saying or doing. Jesus did this when using certain characters or groups in His parables to help His followers or those He was teaching better understand the message. For you it means that you can't teach a Sunday School lesson to children the same way you would adults. Likewise when working with teens, you may have to interject some current slang or drop in references to pop music, trendy web sites or movies in order for them to get what you're saying. If you're with a group of men, maybe you use some sports analogies to score points. What you do or say is not nearly important is what your audience gets out of it. The point is, get Christ's message across however you can and maximize its impact by using language, images and stories you think will resonate strongly with that particular audience or individual. Use whatever works—the bottom line is you want to break through however you can to help them "get it."

There's a growing trend that shows how Christian leaders in the church are taking this notion to heart and adapting Christ's message to reach out and capture the attention of a broader audience, especially teens and young adults. More and more congregations and denominations are adding contemporary worship services on Sunday mornings and on select nights during the week. While these services vary widely from one church to the next, many involve state-of-the-art acoustics and lighting, large video screens, interactive graphics and well-staged theatrics. And with electric and bass guitars, drums and keyboards replacing the traditional piano and organ, many of these services feel more like a rock concert than a worship service. Maybe these contemporary services appeal to you and your family, maybe not. But Christ's message, whether expressed through amped-up music, dramatic skits or modern dance routines, does indeed captivate some who might otherwise choose not to participate in a conventional worship service. To me, whatever gets more people involved in worship and living a life for Christ is a good thing.

There's a delightful stage comedy entitled *Smoke on the Mountain* that's popular in local theater. If you've never seen the play, I encourage you to do so when you have the chance. The play centers on the Sanders family invited to sing and entertain a small church congregation one Saturday night in Mount Pleasant, North Carolina. Not your typical bunch of Christian entertainers, the family belts out old-time Gospel bluegrass hymns on the fiddle, banjo and guitar much to the disdain of two elderly dowagers who find the Sanders' musical liberties and honest, but outrageous testimonials to be not only insulting, but downright sacrilegious. As the play evolves, the pair of crabby curmudgeons slowly but surely find themselves filled with the spirit, stomping their feet and clapping their hands to the music. And, somewhere along the way, they finally seem to accept that the Sanders' down home way of worship, though very much different from their own, is somehow alright.

There's certainly nothing wrong with the "tried and true" ways of worshipping or advertising God. But, to reach out and capture the attention of many of today's non-believers or fringe church worshippers, you have to do something different, especially for those who have the "been there, done that" attitude towards church and worship. You can't always apply the same ol', same ol' or generic cookie cutter approach to worshipping, witnessing and working for Christ. As times change, technology evolves and communities become more diverse, churches and their Christian members need to become more progressive and learn to think outside of the box in order to appeal to a much wider audience. While some congregations will inevitably quibble that such changes are polarizing and divisive, I argue such changes will have the opposite effect. Providing alternatives is actually less exclusionary, not more alienating, which makes more people feel welcome in worship and invites greater participation and involvement within the church.

Like the stodgy old church ladies in *Smoke on the Mountain,* you may not always agree with the delivery of the message, embrace another person's interpretation of Scripture, or approve of the way someone goes about the business of advertising God. But like it or not, as long as what they say or do is Scripturally sound, rooted in core Christian principles and helps draw more people into a covenant relationship Christ, it is something that's worthy of your prayers and support. God gave us creativity for a reason—He wants us to use it! Don't box someone into your way of doing things just because you don't like or understand how they worship, how they hype God or how they bring others to Christ or into key ministry positions.

## 2. Generate Interest

When faced with a buying decision, the typical consumer wants to know "What can this product do for me?" or "How does this product solve my problem?" In order to be successful, advertisers must supply the customer the answers to these questions and give them a reason to buy. It is the advertiser's answers that generate the customer's interest. Some companies cut right to the benefits or great low price. Others create a problem so they can sell a solution. Or, they give a common item a fancy new name to create some product buzz and excitement. Take drop earrings for example. They have been popular for years, but some creative soul in the jewelry industry coined the more upscale phrase "chandelier earrings" to generate new interest and foster the perception of a unique new style. Women, convinced the earrings were the latest and greatest in jewelry, just had to have a pair and sales increased.

Every product may not have a unique selling point, but every product does have something that differentiates it, even if ever so slightly, from its competitor. Think paper towels are just paper towels? Wrong. Bounty is the Quicker-Picker-Upper. What makes Cascade dishwashing detergent better than another brand? Cascade has sheeting action for virtually spotless dishes. And what makes a Chevrolet truck appear better than a Ford or Dodge. A Chevy truck is built like a rock.

These companies successfully generate interest in their wares by creating a positioning statement that reinforces an image of their product as being superior to that offered by a competitor. We may not know exactly what a Hemi engine is, what Retsyn does, or which three out of four dentists recommend a certain gum, but these "advertisisms" sure do sound good and exert some powerful and persuasive influence on our buying decisions.

As a Christian, you too can generate interest or create buzz about God. Before you go into a situation where you'll be advertising God, consider all the accomplishments and benefits God offers. Each of us will approach this with a slightly different perspective and that's okay. Just think, Almighty God created the heavens and earth. He developed all the intricate workings of nature from the tiniest amoebas to the most complex of all living beings, humans. He embodies the word love. He empowers the weak. He heals the afflicted and the diseased. He sent His only Son to rescue us from sin and to bequeath us the gift of eternal life. Additionally, try to anticipate questions and objections others may bring up and jot down answers. You may also want to and arm yourself with relevant Scripture in advance to help you better state your case or make your point.

You also generate interest and create excitement for God when others take notice of the happy and fulfilled Christian life that you live. You stimulate interest when others see and hear you praising and honoring God without hesitation or fear of reprisals and when you glorify and exalt God equally as loud when things are going well and when things aren't going so great. Your praises can help encourage non-believers to seek out Christ's power and grace or inspire believers to reevaluate their own attitude towards and dependency on God. People watch how you cope in certain situations and a positive outlook centered on God helps create a desire in those watching to experience that same kind of spiritual joy and peace you have in Jesus Christ.

One only has to think back to the days following Hurricane Katrina in late August and early September of 2005 to see this kind of unwavering faith in action. Many evacuees I saw interviewed on TV who had lost everything—homes, cars, jobs, pets, even loved ones—still continued praising God, thankful for their own lives and feeling blessed for the little they had left. Yes, they were devastated and uncertain where they would go or what they would do, but the ones I saw never blamed God or expressed anger at Him for their circumstances. They felt the love and compassion of Christ even amid the worst of times and shared that faith with all who were watching the interview.

## 3. Build Desire

Building desire is simply piquing someone's curiosity about a product, or in our case, about God. Advertisers build desire by tantalizing us with phrases such as "stop in for a test drive," "taste our new flavors," "get your free sample today" and by teasing us with ads that hint of a new product or store coming to town.

You build desire for God by the language you use, the people you associate with, the projects you get involved with, the deeds you do. In Matthew 5:14,

Jesus declares you are the light of the world. Pay close attention to Jesus' words here. You are not *a light,* you are *the light.* If you want to build desire in people you can't live in the shadows. People like to see what they're getting into, and when they see you living proudly in the light of Christ, they get a good look at what being a true Christian is all about.

Like it or not, that means much attention is focused on you, the things you say and the things you do. If you live inconsistently with what you profess, people notice your hypocrisy and duplicity. The light you have that could have been so influential and appealing to others is suddenly dimmed and the promising message you bring is tuned out. Think how many times you've heard people who don't attend church say they were turned off by Christians who said one thing but did the total opposite. Or the times someone at your office or school expressed surprise that you are a Christian. It makes you wonder what you say or do that would make them come to that conclusion, doesn't it?

As Christians, we need to make Christ the brightest spot in our life. That means putting less emphasis on money, material possessions, hobbies and anything else that darkens our relationship with Christ. As the light of God, you have three distinct choices. You can choose to shine brightly in the world and illuminate others to the love and grace of Jesus Christ. You can choose to barely glow so as not to give off much light at all. Or worse, you can remain the burned out light that leaves you and all the ones you encounter in spiritual darkness.

Years ago, I read that in every culture, from the most civilized to the most primitive, sociologists discovered there is generally an innate belief in the existence of a creator, and almost always, in some sort of afterlife. While the creator is known by many different names (most of which are not synonymous with the one true God we worship), the recognition exists among all peoples that there is something much bigger than any of them at work in the universe.

I mention this because humans come equipped with a natural curiosity to learn more about their creator. In other words, the desire is already there. All you have to do is arouse interest, tap into it and build an insatiable desire for the one true living God.

The ways you can accomplish this are as infinite as your imagination. For example, you can build desire about God simply by listening to another's problem and offering advice or directing them to specific verses in the Bible you feel are beneficial to them and their situation. You build desire by sharing your own faith story or telling others how God brought you through a particularly rough time. You build desire by putting your faith into action, volunteering for a faith-based disaster relief project, giving someone a religious-themed book or starting up a new church ministry. All these things pique genuine curiosity about Christ for those who don't know God, those who have drifted away from Him or those who want to reconnect with Christ. Such actions on your part are outward, visible and tangible signs of your love for Christ.

Another way to build desire for God is by tapping into one's aspirations. Corporate advertisers and cataloguers cleverly position their products in such a way that makes customers aspire to be part of the lifestyle, luxury and success their advertising imagery and products promote. Such ads conjure up positive thoughts like I want to be like slim and trim like that woman, I wish I drove a luxury sedan like that, I want my home to be as well-decorated as the one in that magazine photo, I want to save my boss money on shipping costs, and I want my body to be as tone and sculpted as the guy working out on that home gym.

As one who strives to live an obedient life in Jesus Christ, you are called and challenged by God to create that same semblance of desire and aspiration within others. Shower them with encouragement and help get them to the place where they're saying I want to be more like Christ, I want to find a way to better serve my church, I want to teach Sunday School, I want to help lead others to Christ, I want to use my spiritual gifts for the good of God.

So where can you find such folks in which to build all that desire? Well for one thing, stop looking solely inside the church. Sinners and those yearning to establish a relationship with God aren't always seated in the church pews on Sunday mornings. Advertising God may require you to take your light and go into dark alleyways, jails, homeless shelters, third world countries and other less than desirable places many would just assume avoid. If you're truly committed to sharing God's message and furthering His kingdom, however, that dedication to Christ may mean stepping away the certainty and security of your comfort zone and going into places where people on the fringe feel more at ease in their element. I love the way Bishop Eddie Long, pastor of New Birth Missionary Baptist Church, describes it. He says, "One of the things we have lost in the church is that we have to catch the fish before we clean them."[9] Whenever you build desire in someone and encourage or persuade them to reach out for Christ, you become the fisher of men that Jesus desires you to be.

## 4. Motivate Action and Close the Sale

While advertising God can be quick, it can't be rushed. When you advertise God, you can't just speak a few words, say a fast prayer, or rattle off a Bible verse or two and expect to be done with it. You have to invest a little more time than that. It's the same way with advertising. One-time ads in business don't generally pull well and one-time mentions don't work so well when you're promoting God either.

Consider your own reaction to the advertisements you encounter. The first time you see or read an ad, it may not motivate or interest you because you're not in the right frame of mind or in the market for the item being advertised. But maybe the second, third or twentieth time you see, read or hear that same ad does the trick. People respond to repetition and generally need some further prodding or enticement before they're spurred to action.

Companies who advertise also stress a sense of urgency to heighten interest and motivate a swift buying decision on your end. Why do you think TV ads urge you to hurry because supplies are limited or encourage you to order in the next 15 minutes to receive a free gift or promotional discount? Or, how often do you hear the words "be there early, doors open at 8 a.m." or "get here quick, sale ends Monday?" These companies are prompting decisive and immediate action on your part. They want you to buy, call, click a web link, or schedule a test drive ASAP after seeing or hearing their ad. Companies realize the longer you wait, the less likely you are to respond and purchase.

When advertising God, it's up to you to initiate that same kind of call to action. In other words, you want the person who interacts with your message to do something. You want them to come to church or bring a friend to Sunday school *next week*. You want them to sign up *today* to help out on that church service project you're chairing. You want them to seize hold of their spiritual gift *this instant* and put it to good use for God. You want them to *start now* reading the Bible and praying more.

And because you want to create urgency, there's absolutely nothing wrong with a little follow up, or what I like to call persistent persuasion. As long as unbelievers or uninvolved Christians are out there procrastinating and making excuses, the less likely they are to seek out Christ or participate in His work. I'm not advocating that you pester someone to death, but you can't afford to be passive either. Passivity can be misconstrued as indifference or a lack of caring on your part. Being persistent shows you care. Don't send mixed messages. Be proactive when advertising God and repetitive in your calls for them to put Christ first and foremost in their life. It's cliché I know, but if only one person accepts Christ or enters into a deeper spiritual relationship with Him as a direct result of something you said or did, it is well worthy of your effort.

## Results May Not Come in the Timely Manner You Expect

In real life, things don't usually happen overnight or as fast as you want them to. Many corporate advertisers share the same lament. After their ad runs, some of them have grand visions of inventory flying off the shelves or phones ringing off the hook with orders, only to be disappointed when there's only a minimal spike in sales. Because their expectations aren't based in reality and sights are set too high, they experience a let down.

As you advertise God, it's easy to harbor unrealistic expectations of things you want to happen as well. So when people with whom you've advertised God are not spurred to action or their verbal support and promise to get involved doesn't translate to enthusiastic participation, it's easy to experience a let down after being on such an emotional high for God.

Don't, however, let me discourage you from expecting Christ to deliver results when you do His work. In fact, you should fully expect and pray that He will. It's not unreasonable for you to want to see a neighbor at church after extending an invitation. To anticipate calls and e-mails from people wanting to go on a mission trip after you've made the announcement. To want friends and family to kick bad habits and addictions and never relapse. To expect to be a witness to miraculous healing.

Just be aware that when you advertise God, tangible, quantifiable results sometimes may not come for a long time, if at all. You can't worry about that. Don't get all wrapped up in what happens, what doesn't happen or what you want to happen. And don't focus on unrealistic expectations or become overly optimistic about an outcome. Do what God asks, then leave the rest up to Him.

Let me share a story about misplaced perception, expectation and the reality of Christ being in control. As a teenager growing up in a Southern Baptist church in Roswell, Georgia, I was amazed week after week at how our preacher, Pastor Dick as we called him, always drew the sermon's benediction out as long as possible to give anyone interested in getting saved a chance to come forward.

When Pastor Dick's sermons were particularly emotional, beads of perspiration would bubble up on his forehead, which he would deftly wipe away with the folded white handkerchief he always clutched in his hand. As he invited the congregation to sing every verse of the hymns *Just As I Am* or *I Surrender All,* he would passionately exhort anyone who was without Christ to walk down that center aisle and find Him. Sometimes between song verses, Pastor Dick would ask the pianist to stop playing and he would encourage the unsaved to come now. "Don't wait until next week," he would plead. "Come now while we sing this last verse." Sometimes, people took those last few moments to come forward, take hold of Pastor Dick's hand and tearfully confess their heartfelt desire to accept Christ. Someone accepting his plea to come always seemed to bring him great joy.

But on the days when no one came, I remember Pastor Dick looking tired and defeated as if he had poured every ounce of energy he had into that benediction to no avail. Because I expected droves of unbelievers to walk down the aisle and accept Christ, I imagined Pastor Dick feeling like he must have wasted a good sermon because there were no tangible results from his efforts. Looking back now, I know I was wrong. Pastor Dick's words weren't wasted on anyone. I'm sure his message created a desire for Christ in someone each and every week. They didn't need to walk down the aisle to validate the effectiveness of Pastor Dick's sermon. They could have easily phoned him the next day and made arrangements to talk, or perhaps his message planted a seed of faith in them that materialized months or years later.

Like Pastor Dick's impassioned sermons, your message can be a powerful motivator and provide great inspiration, but it doesn't necessarily mean people are going to jump right on your invitation to accept Christ, come to church with you, join your Bible study or sign up to be on that stewardship or missionary committee. Instead of allowing frustration and feelings of failure to set in, recognize that circumstances beyond your control may be at work and that it could take several invitations or ongoing encouragement before an acceptance is given.

It's okay to have goals and objectives. But, if those goals and objectives are not met within the specific time frame you've set in your own mind or marked on your calendar, don't consider your efforts wasted or grow hesitant advertising God in similar situations in the future. Become more like the advertiser I just talked about. Be patient and give your audience time to come around and get comfortable with the message you're sharing. Salespeople call this cultivating a relationship. Ask anyone in sales and they'll tell you that it's not unusual to call on a prospect for months or years before finally brokering a deal or signing a big contract.

It's sort of the same principle when you advertise God. Sometimes you have to cultivate those relationships and, depending on that person's mindset and willingness to get more involved, it can take time to move them from prospective Christian wannabe or Sunday only worshipper into the role of active, faithful Christian. Whether you see the fruits of your spiritual labors or not, you did what God called you to do when you seized those advertising God moments.

The reasons why people don't respond to advertising God are too numerous and varied to list. Most of the time it isn't anything you say or do that turns them off. And it's never a situation where God under-delivers. Persons who are consistently unyielding to the call of Christ generally do so out their own pride, indifference or stubbornness. God gives them the free will to make a choice and sometimes that choice won't be what you hope for or expect.

So you don't get the immediate and visible results you expect. It can be disappointing and frustrating because you want to see results from your efforts in order to have that sense of accomplishment. But are you a failure because you advertised God or did the work He called you to do? Absolutely not! You may feel like it's that way in your own mind due to a poor reception or an unenthusiastic response, but God doesn't see it that way. You've successfully done what He calls you to do and for that you should be proud even if the results aren't noticeable right away.

Remember, too, that God doesn't work off your timetable. Being omnipotent and omnipresent as He is, God is in the best place to decide what to do and when to do it. Sometimes His actions are quick. Sometimes it may take a long time before anything happens. Your words or actions today could very well be the springboard that gets something going down the road. Whether it's months, years or even decades later, people may recall the time you advertised God as a watershed moment in their life and may very well cite your action as the catalyst that steered them in a more Godly direction. Maybe you can point to a moment like that in your own life as well. If so, share the story sometime—it's a great way to advertise God!

*Advertising God in Real Life:*

*Tom is a coworker who also lives in Dave's area. One day over lunch, Tom casually remarks he was once an avid guitar player, but now with a wife and kids, he rarely has time to play. Dave knows his church is always looking for talented musicians to participate in Sunday morning's contemporary worship service. Since Tom lives nearby, Dave invites Tom and his family to check out the service at Dave's church. Maybe, suggests Dave, if Tom enjoys the service, he could audition to play guitar one or two Sundays a month with the band. Also knowing Tom is unchurched, Dave feels this is a subtle way of getting Tom into church without being too forward or pushy. But Tom always politely declines Dave's invites, making excuses why he just can't make it.*

*One day, Dave discovers Tom has been promoted and must relocate out of state. While shaking hands with Tom on Tom's last day, Dave mentions he really wishes*

*Tom had gotten a chance to play in the church band. Dave encourages Tom to find a church in his new community and pick up playing the guitar again.*

*Months later, while strumming his guitar, Tom recalls Dave's supportive words and all those invitations to church. Tom decides to give church a try and begins asking around in his neighborhood about churches that have a contemporary worship service. Tom and his family visit a local church one Sunday and enjoy it immensely. Before long, Tom is a regular musician in the worship service, and soon afterwards, Tom and his family commit their lives to Christ, are baptized and join the church. Tom always remembers Dave fondly, telling friends if it weren't for the persistent urgings of his coworker, he knew he wouldn't be in church now and that guitar of his would still be gathering dust in the closet.*

*Though he never knows the results of his actions, Dave advertises God by encouraging an unchurched friend to pursue his spiritual gift and to get involved in the church.*

## Things Don't Always Turn Out Like You Plan, But Things Always Turn Out Like God Plans

Consider again Jesus' parable of the sower in Matthew 13:1-23. Some who hear Christ's message won't understand it, nor will they be inclined to delve into it any further. They eventually return to their old ways without repenting or accepting Christ. Others who hear will gladly take your words to heart and maybe even accept Christ, but they steadily fall away when troubles come along because their faith is too weak. Still others will come to Christ, but then they allow worry, career ambitions, leisurely pursuits and other life distractions to render them ineffective and unproductive Christians. A smaller group will hear and accept the words of Christ, take the message to heart and re-direct their life and goals to be in harmony with God's plans. They live by the Scriptures, study the Bible, pray daily and become productive believers for God.

It's impossible for you to predict which group those who see and hear you advertising God will fall into. As a Christian following and obeying God, you can't be responsible for what people do with the information given to them. Like the rich young man Jesus encountered who refused to part with his wealth and join Christ's discipleship, God knows every person who hears His message isn't going to accept it. Even people who heard Christ preach and saw the miracles He performed rejected Him. It's no different now. People choose to either accept or reject the invitation of Jesus Christ. They can't waffle back and forth. They either remain shackled to a sinful, unrepentant lifestyle that draws them away from God or find redemption, restoration and salvation in Christ and in living a faithful, productive life for Him.

This kind of indecision makes me think of the young, pretty single girl romantically involved in a fairly so-so relationship. She's with a guy who's fairly good-looking, has a fairly decent job and treats her fairly nice. She's just not 100% sure whether he's the man of her dreams or just some guy she can get by with. One day, she meets another man who is better looking, has a better job and treats her nicer. She likes him a lot too, but rather than risk the fairly safe thing she has with bachelor #1 and take a chance on greater happiness with bachelor #2, she remains content to stay with bachelor #1 because she's fairly happy and comfortable there. In other words bachelor #2, great as he may be, is simply not worth the risk. In her mind, why even take a chance?

Some who see or hear you advertising God are just like the pretty girl. They want to stay right where they are in life because they're safe and comfortable there. People like this are wary of risking all they perceive they have in exchange for a potential greater joy they feel reasonably sure they would find in God. They want to make the change and know deep down that they should, but yet they can't. In their mind, the risk versus reward factor is too iffy to chance. So they pass on God and are left beholden to worldly things that are fairly attractive and nice, but things that don't create true happiness, optimism and satisfaction like forsaking it all for God brings. And it's not just unbelievers. There's plenty of Christians who have a hard time kicking some of their own sinful baggage and so-so relationships to the curb as well.

As you go about advertising God you're going to meet with some resistance and not everyone will be persuaded today, tomorrow or ever by what you say or do. But you know what? There are plenty of others who will be moved by your words and actions and they will act on it in their own time.

It's the same way with advertising. The results of a great ad aren't always immediate. In advertising, the rule of seven states that it takes multiple exposures to a specific ad before a consumer will connect with its message and content. And that's okay. The advertiser is branding their name and creating familiarity with their product each and every time you see or hear their ad. They are patient, realizing the pay off of your purchase may happen weeks or even months down the road.

So don't worry about response rates to your message. In the eyes of God, your confidence and character as a Christian witness is not validated by the action or inaction of others. And you don't know what God has planned later on for them. It's the Christians who faithfully and proactively sow the seeds of change today that make it possible for others to give their lives to Christ, re-energize and rejuvenate their relationship with Jesus, or do amazing things in the Lord's name later on.

You may never see the spiritual outcome of your efforts and endeavors, may never know about it, may never directly benefit from it, but you had a part in it because you were courageous and confident enough to advertise God yesterday, a few months ago, or even decades back. It's not the time that's important, but the timing. You were there with that "here I am" attitude when God wanted you to say or do something and you did it. That's the important part—doing something—because the outcome of your actions is often beyond your control. That's why when you become more God-oriented instead of results-oriented, you're better able to consistently live out and express your own faith and free yourself up to let God do His thing after you do yours.

## UP FOR DISCUSSION.

1. In your opinion, what's the "hook" of God's message? How can we get unbelievers and fringe worshippers to pay attention to it?

2. What are some ads that captured your attention and why? What are some of the cues you could take from today's ads to help you better promote God?

3. How would you answer the question, "What does God do for me?" How would you go about generating interest for God?

4. How can we build aspiration and motivate action for Jesus Christ on the part of others?

5. Is it important for you to personally see results when you advertise God? Why or why not? How does it make you feel if no visible, tangible results occur?

# 7

# *Competition and Advertising God*

○ ○ ○ ○ ○ ○ ○ ○ ○ ○ ○ ○ ○ ○ ○ ○ ○ ○ ○ ○ ○ ○ ○ ○ ○ ○ ○ ○ ○ ○ ○

"Set your minds on things above, not on earthly things."

—{ *Colossians 3:2* }

In a free market society, healthy and robust competition between opposing companies is beneficial to all. Among other things, active and sustained competition helps foster innovation, create jobs, improve quality and customer service, and keep prices in check. But, while competition may be good for business here on earth, it's an unwanted distraction in the business of advertising God. For clarity purposes, I'm defining competition as those things that preclude or distract us from responding or reacting to our Lord and Savior Jesus Christ.

Think of it this way. Christ teaches us to make God our #1 priority, so it only makes sense that anything that competes for our attention ultimately diverts us from focusing entirely on God. Ours is a fast-paced world to be sure, but God shouldn't have to compete for our attention. The reality is, however, that too often God has to pry our attention away from one thing to help us concentrate on another. Some people will comply, but many will resist His nudge because they're quite happily distracted away from God and don't want their attention focused anywhere else. No wonder when it comes to serving God and living a Christ-focused life, competition becomes a dangerous diversion for Christians wanting to put God first.

Those who successfully advertise God won't ignore nor discount that competition either. Rather, these types of Christians learn to recognize competition for what it really is—a deceitful tactic used by Satan to undermine and ultimately defeat their attempts to share the good news of Jesus Christ with others.

And don't think for one second Satan is not trying to distract you and get you off task. Competition is as fierce in the spiritual world as it is in the corporate world. Think about all the things that compete with Jesus in your own life. What are some of the ways you get distracted from praying, reading the Bible, worshipping, sharing testimony or getting involved in an area of need? Is it a "must-see TV" night? Your career ambitions? Time-consuming hobbies or leisurely pursuits? None of these things is necessarily bad in and of themselves, but they become unhealthy frivolity when you prioritize them over God.

Like all the distractions secular advertising must overcome, there are many obstacles and impediments that prevent your Christian voice and spiritual message from being seen, heard and acted upon, too. In a perfect world, promoting and talking about God would be easy for anyone whose life has been transformed by the magnificent love and saving grace of Jesus Christ. Christians would be so pumped up for Christ that they would constantly praise Him and be willing to do anything and go anywhere for Christ. They would be proud of their salvation and wouldn't care what others thought or said about them. But, a perfect world ours is not. Inevitably, distractions come our way and the duty of advertising God can—and often does—get easily pushed to the back burner.

God doesn't value competition for His attention. In fact, He abhors it. Just take a look at the very first commandment—you shall have no other gods before me. Putting that commandment first tells you the importance God places on it. So why is it so many Christians continue to place other "gods" first? Let's take a look at a few of the more common "competitions" that distract us, get us off track and weaken our dependency on God and our ability to passionately promote Him and the good things He wants us to pursue.

## Money, Money, Money

Some say the real measure of wealth is how much you would be worth if you lost all your money. In the classic film *It's A Wonderful Life,* Jimmy Stewart's character George Bailey experiences this reality firsthand when he's threatened with shame, bankruptcy and even jail time when a large sum of money from his business is accidentally lost. I'm sure you know the story. Feeling desperate and like a complete failure in life, George wishes he had never been born, until his guardian angel Clarence shows George just how wonderful his life really is. In the final heartwarming scene, George is surrounded by loved ones and toasted by his brother Harry, who declares George to be the richest man in town. George Bailey didn't warrant that moniker because of his material fortunes, but because of the wealth of love showered upon him by his family and friends in his time of need.

Like George Bailey, far too many people determine their worth by the amount of money or success they have and this causes them to lose sight of what's really valuable like family, friendships and spirituality. And instead of placing value on the relationship they build and nurture with God, these people are more likely gauge their life's success by the size of their stock portfolio, the prestige name adorning their vehicles, and the zip code or square footage of their house.

And for those who tend to put more trust and faith in wealth than they do in God, money becomes the "god" they inevitably put first. Thanks to the alluring promises of secular advertising, far too many Christians unintentionally gravitate towards the worship of wealthy lifestyles and all its trappings. And somewhere along the way, they come to the very wrong conclusion that money affords them more satisfaction, more security and more comfort than investing in a long-term relationship with Jesus Christ. Things haven't changed much from the apostle Paul's day. In 1 Timothy 6:17, Paul charges his student Timothy to teach others "not to put their hope in wealth, which is so uncertain, but to put their hope in God, who richly provides us with everything for our enjoyment."

Money competes against and distracts us from God probably more than any other single item. But money itself is not the core problem. After all, money provides us with the basic necessities of life and affords us certain freedoms and luxuries that come from hard work and financial discipline. But money only becomes "the root of all evil," as Paul refers to it in Timothy, when you use it selfishly or elevate its value and worth over your dependency on God.

Money also corrupts when you view it as something that you earned and deserve as opposed to a reward God has blessed you with. True, you did the hard work to earn that paycheck, but it is God who gifted you with the skill and talent to do what you do for a living. Instead of counting dollars and cents, learn to count your spiritual blessings and heap thanks and praise upon God for all He has richly provided you.

Don't be like the rich young man who approached Jesus and wanted to know how he could get to heaven. Jesus, knowing of the man's great fortune, told him to go sell everything he had and give the money to the poor. The Bible says the man went away sad because he knew he couldn't bear to part with all his money. He obviously felt more secure surrounded by the trappings of his vast wealth than in the merciful arms of Christ.

Isn't that the way it is with many Christians today? We serve and follow God up to a point, but when it interferes with or threatens to take too much of our money or time, we back off to protect our assets instead of promoting God at all costs. Or when it comes time to tithe, we'd rather eat lunch out, save up for that new plasma HDTV and dream vacation, or fatten our savings account rather than cut back and make genuine sacrifices to give the full 10% God requires or donate dollars to a worthwhile church endeavor. Spiritual priorities are out of whack when we feel safer and more secure with that money in our pocket instead of faithfully and dutifully portioning out some of our earnings for God.

Let's face it. No matter how much your household income may be, giving a full 10% back to God isn't always easy since everyone's debt to income ratio is proportionate to earnings. Money puts a roof over our head, food on the table and clothes on our backs. It funds our retirement and our kids' college funds. It affords us certain comforts, luxuries and freedoms. With bills, a mortgage, car payments and other monthly obligations, many families live prudently paycheck to paycheck and find it difficult to part with two, five or ten percent of their income, much less a steady church offering. And, some families that can spare the extra money are reluctant to do so because they worry about a tenuous job situation, rising gas prices and healthcare costs or unexpected household or vehicle repairs.

But how many times have you heard testimony from fellow worshippers or read stories where God's promise has been revealed in someone's life? It's inspiring and reassuring to know that God not only knows and satisfies our needs, but also in some cases, exceeds our needs and wants beyond our wildest expectations. Years ago, my grandparents had to declare bankruptcy and were relegated to a fixed income that was substantially less than the monies to which they were accustomed. But every month, my grandfather faithfully honored his tithe and wrote a check to the church. Both my grandparents advertised their love for Christ by putting more trust in their relationship with God than in the little bit of money they had in the bank. To me, that was powerful testimony, and although my grandparents were proud people and would have never mentioned this to others, I think had people heard their story, they would have been moved by their devotion to God in spite of their financial situation. I can't recall any dramatic blessings in my grandparents' lives explicitly created by their faithful tithing, but I'll bet you they could share plenty of momentous ways in which God blessed them over the years. Blessings that may seem insignificant to you and I but were pronounced and memorable in their lives.

Once you loosen up the purse strings and cheerfully give back to God, expect to be blessed. I love the Scripture from Malachi 3:10 where God proclaims, "Bring the whole tithe into the storehouse, that there may be food in my house. Test me in this," says the Lord Almighty, "and see if I will not throw open the floodgates of heaven and pour out so much blessing that you will not have room enough for it."

Be careful in your interpretation of Malachi's verse however. Tithing and giving offerings to God are not intended to be tit for tat. Don't get caught up in which blessings you or others may receive. The blessings may not always come in the form of monetary or material possessions or even come in your lifetime. Only God knows what those blessings will be and when they will be poured out. Give cheerfully because you love the Lord and strive to obey all His commands, not because you expect to be "repaid" dollar for dollar with spiritual blessings.

In Matthew 6:19-21, Jesus warns "Do not store up for yourselves treasures on earth…but store up for yourselves treasures in heaven…for where your treasure is, there your heart will be also." When you feel like you're putting more trust and faith into money than into God, go to Him in prayer. Confess your sin and ask God to forgive you for turning money into a "god" and to help you become less reliant on the almighty dollar and more dependent on Almighty God.

## Career Ambitions

Susan spent her whole adult life trying to make it to the top. She worked 12 hours days, frequently came into the office on weekends, and even sacrificed relationships and vacation time to further her career. Work was her passion and she poured everything she had into it to achieve her goals. Finally, at the age of 37, she ascended to the presidency of a national media company. When a severe car accident put Susan on long-term disability to recover, she spent all those long and lonely hours alone in bed taking stock of her life (or lack thereof as she joked to herself), especially after a coworker reacquainted Susan with God during her prolonged hospital stay. Though she was often involved in high profile corporate buyouts and mergers, Susan realized how negligent she'd been acquiring the love and forgiveness of Christ in her own life.

Isn't that how it is with some of us? We invest more time, concentration and energy into building a business or growing a career than we do brokering an equitable or symbiotic relationship with God that will last infinitely longer than any of our secular dealings in this life. Our quest for success becomes an unintended competitor with God when we allow our job to take priority over serving, worshipping and selflessly following God.

I realize most of us have to do work of some kind in order to provide for our families and ourselves. Working hard for the buck we earn and enjoying the benefits of success is the American way, after all. But like money, it's not the job itself that creates the negative influence or competition, it's the worth you place on that job or the succeed-at-all-costs mentality some have about their career that starts to cause spiritual problems. Some people claim their relationship with God is not one that's "me-focused," but the way they continue to put God second, third or even fourth indicates otherwise.

For instance, the title on your office door or the nature of your work makes you become arrogant and less humble because it gives you a certain status in life or allows you to travel in certain circles that you wouldn't otherwise enjoy. You may also be the classic workaholic who feels as though your job is so integral to your identity that you'll sacrifice everything else to keep it, including your family, your free time, even your church and worship obligations. Or maybe everything you do is done selfishly in the hopes of receiving some financial reward, promotional incentive or recognition for your business.

Let your job be a part of your life, not your life. When you're old and gray, you're not likely to look back and wish you'd spent more time at the office, made more money or brokered more deals to fatten the company's bottom line. No, most of us I think, will look back with regrets—that we didn't eat dinner as a family more, didn't go on that dream vacation, didn't spend more time doing what God wanted us to do. We can't take that promotion, that nice corner office or that big expense account with us when we die. What we can take with us is the pride and satisfaction of being a loyal Christian servant and a faithful worshipper who didn't let money or work compete with God and distract us from the command of the Great Commission.

## Leisurely Pursuits

Maybe it's not your money or job that interferes with you doing God's work, but your leisure and recreational activities. If you're a young up and comer or the workaholic who's busy climbing the corporate ladder, coming in early, staying late and putting in sixty hours a week, the weekends are precious. Maybe you reserve Sunday mornings for brunch with friends, jogging in the park or just sleeping late.

For couples with children, weeknights can be filled with school functions, club events and sports practices, while weekend afternoons are spent shuttling your little stars to their soccer and baseball games. Or to spend more time with the family, you're one who likes to jaunt off on weekend getaways, buy season tickets to professional sporting events, or spend all your spare time boating and fishing at the lake.

None of these activities is inherently bad and I'm not saying you shouldn't enjoy your life and all the good things that come with it. God wants you to enjoy life. Like money or your career though, recreational activities only become a problem when you put precedence on them over God. It's also a problem when you use them as veiled excuses to justify why you can't help out here or do that there in the church or when you're unable to sacrifice the things you want to do in favor of what God wants you to do.

## Clutter, Clutter Everywhere

One of the frequent complaints among advertisers is that there's too much "noise," or clutter, in people's lives. This clutter not only creates distraction, but also often causes people to miss the advertiser's message completely. Every corporate advertiser must find a way to successfully combat and overcome competition that inhibits the receipt of the advertised message. Advertisers have to compete with other ads, fleeting attention spans, skepticism and mistrust, as well as other businesses that are selling the same or similar goods and services. And, if all that wasn't enough to turn an advertiser's hair gray, should their message actually catch your attention, it has but a precious few seconds to hold it long enough to persuade you to purchase. Little wonder so many advertisements fail to generate enough revenue to cover their costs.

For Christians advertising God, clutter is often competition you will face when sharing Christ's message, too. The notoriously brief and fickle attention spans we all seem to possess cause us to hit sensory overload pretty quickly sometimes. And when people get to that point, they are far less likely to respond or react to someone's words or call to action when they're advertising God. That's exactly why corporate advertisers run the same ad at different hours of the day hoping the message catches you at a good time when your attention is more focused and less distracted.

As frustrating as all these distractions can be when advertising God to other people, I think God could easily make the same complaint when He's trying to communicate with us. Think about how often you're too distracted or too involved with other things to focus entirely on God. You feel like He wants you to do this or do that, but you are inundated with a variety of mixed messages from your family, friends, coworkers, maybe even from your own conscience that convolutes the true message. You can get so confused that you're not sure what to do so you procrastinate, waffle back and forth and waste time and opportunities through your indecision.

You also get so preoccupied with the daily happenings in your own life and those of your family that you sometimes miss God's calling altogether or simply aren't receptive to hearing and responding to His voice at this particular moment in time. And no wonder. In the course of a normal day, the average person is subjected to dozens of different messages from TV and radio commercials to billboards and bus signs to newspaper and magazine ads. You ignore the majority of these ads because you are not in the mindset to purchase whatever it is the advertiser is selling at this time. The message has no meaning or relevance to you.

But say you are in the market for a new car. Ads for new cars garner some attention because your interest is already heightened and you are more receptive to being advertised to. However, once you narrow the buying selection to a specific make or model, many of those same ads will lose impact because you're no longer considering particular vehicle makes and models.

It's the same way with non-believers and those who've stepped back from God or fallen away from the church. Sometimes the message you share with these people will not resonate. It doesn't mean they didn't hear or appreciate what you had to say, that they're totally blowing you off, or even discounting your words. Your message is filtered out because they aren't currently in the "market" for God's services.

Does that mean you should throw up your hands in defeat and move on to another who might be more receptive to God's message? Absolutely not! Remember, repetition is key. It can take multiple exposures to a message before there's measurable impact on the audience, so don't give up if someone tunes you out or doesn't bite on the message. Take a cue from the advertiser's handbook and try, try again to get God's message across. Here's an insider's hint. Advertising research indicates people are more receptive to receiving information in the morning hours. Try using that little nugget to your advantage when advertising God.

In Matthew 18:21-22, Peter approaches Jesus and asks how many times he should forgive someone who has wronged him. Jewish teachers in Jesus' day instructed that three times was enough, so Peter, thinking he is being generous, asks if seven times is sufficient. Jesus answers seventy-seven times, which I take to mean forgive someone more times than you can count.

I think the same principle applies when you're hyping God to people who seemingly tune you out or have no interest. You can't put a number on how many times you "re-air" the message. You should persistently advertise God like Jesus teaches you to forgive—a countless number of times or as long as it takes to convince someone that Jesus Christ is indeed the way, the truth and the life. Keep in mind this is another one of those situations where you may not see tangible results from your efforts now or ever. But focus on the bigger picture. It's not near as important that you actually see results as it is that you get out there and share God's word with those who need to hear it.

Also, if and when someone tunes you out or is non-responsive, don't give up, talk bad about them to others, or out of shame, anger or both, avoid them whenever they come around. Remain positive, confident and above all, persistent. And when I say persistent, I'm not talking about badgering a person. It's the same kind of persistence I talked about earlier—being the faithful constant that keeps God's word and promises in front of that person and letting them know that you care about their life and spiritual well being. Patiently sticking with someone over the long haul reveals a loving heart. The Christ-like care and compassion you display serves as a visible witness to others who observe your God-first attitude in action.

## Don't Believe You Can't, Have Faith You Can

Competition also comes from the naysayers in our lives. These are the pessimists who always tell you why something can't be done or denigrate ideas that they deem won't work. It makes me think of an animated cartoon series called Gulliver's Travels that my brothers and I regularly watched as children. One character, appropriately named Glum, was the classic pessimist. Every week, Gulliver and his band of little people would inevitably find themselves in a dangerous or precarious situation. One of them would always have a great idea on how to solve the problem or escape from dire circumstances. But, week after week, it was always the ever-gloomy Glum who could only see failure instead of success, futility instead of triumph. Is there a Glum or two in your life? Don't let their negative attitude and pessimism put impediments or mental roadblocks in front of you. That's just another way Satan tries to stop you from doing good things for God. Stand strong in your faith, emphasize the positives and allow God to work through you.

There's always going to be Glums in your life telling you why you can't do this, why you can't say that, or why this and that won't work. But why be influenced by them when you can be encouraged by the mighty power of God in the challenges you face? God isn't bound by human limitations nor does He adhere to expectations imposed on Him by the pessimist or skeptic. What if someone had convinced Moses he couldn't possibly lead the Israelites out of Egyptian captivity? What if Noah had listened to all those who thought building the ark was foolishness? What if members of the early church chose to believe in the implausibility of Christ rising from the grave instead of the glory of everlasting life with Him?

*Advertising God in Real Life:*

*Though her husband Ed strongly advises against it, Janine decides to participate in a 32 week Bible study that requires her to attend a two hour class every Sunday night, plus read her Bible and spend time in prayer for about 30 minutes a day, six days a week. Janine and her husband both work full-time and have two elementary-age sons. Ed's long commute requires that he leave very early in the day, so Janine's mornings are hectic what with getting the kids up, bathed, dressed and fed for school. The boys are also involved in after-school and sports activities during the week and on the weekends. After work, Janine likes to spend time with her family, plus she's tired from a long day at the office. The Bible study is a big time commitment and Ed selfishly fears Janine has way too much on her plate. Ed is unsupportive and has no problem letting her know that he doesn't think she can handle it.*

*Undeterred, Janine is determined to successfully complete the program even though she knows her schedule is chockfull. She tells Ed she's willing to get up earlier in the mornings or eat lunch at her desk so she can read her daily lessons and pray then.*

*Janine advertises God by shrugging off Ed's negativity, readjusting her busy schedule and participating in an eight month Bible study despite her husband's objections.*

## You Can't Talk About That!

There's an old adage that says you shouldn't talk politics or religion with family, friends, clients and coworkers for fear of stirring up controversy or arguing over opposing points of view. I say, so what if someone hears your take on faith and Scripture and a healthy debate breaks out. Anytime we're talking about God is a good thing, especially when discussions are grounded in Biblical truth. I think far too many of us take that not-talking-about-religion part way too seriously, almost as if it's a mandate, a self-imposed no-no that dictates we can never talk faith, values and religion outside of the safety zone of the church or church-sponsored gatherings.

I'm sure this kind of thinking makes absolutely no sense to God. When Jesus preached and expressed ideas, it didn't matter which crowd He was among or where His location was. Jesus took risks and preached in places where He and His message were not always welcome nor particularly well received. But instead of stepping aside and moving on, He engaged in Scriptural discussions and challenged others on the validity of their own beliefs.

Likewise, God doesn't intend for faithful, obedient believers to put their lamp under a bowl or shine it only in those places that are safe and convenient, or where you think you'll face the least amount of resistance. You have to consider what's best for God instead of hanging on to what's best for yourself.

One way you do that is by not restricting yourself to the do's and don'ts of advertising God established by humans. You know some of the ones I'm talking about. Speak only about God when asked to. Don't bring up religious issues in business settings. Do follow the tried and true ways of the church. Don't waste your time serving or addressing this group or that one. Do tread lightly when talking about God so no one is offended. Don't impose your views on others of different faiths.

Rather than confront a spiritual issue, answer a theological question or challenge someone's beliefs and risk making waves, it's often easier to stay silent and move on. But, loving Christ should be like a great story we can't wait to tell everyone we know. Instead of cringing at the idea of talking about God, Christians should wish conversations involving Jesus Christ would come up more often. The very mention of His name in casual conversation gives us an "in" from which we can jump in and advertise God. Think of it as the break you've been looking for to get in there and promote God in your own unique style. It's not like you have to do something big and dramatic, give a sermon or be confrontational, just say something, anything that affirms your faith and devotion to Jesus Christ. Seemingly benign, but potentially very powerful, it's just a way you let others know you are a proud follower of Jesus Christ and that you don't care who knows it.

So instead of backing down or cowering in silence like Satan wants you to do (and rejoices when you do I'm sure), actively assume the role of advertiser and consider this your perfect chance to confidently state your position like God wants you to. Okay, so some of those who see or hear you will tune you out, but maybe, just maybe, a few others will take a listen to what you're saying and react accordingly, giving themselves fully to Christ at some point based on your intervention. Perhaps the words you speak will serve as a positive influence and act as a stimulus for change. Perhaps yours are finally the words that break through their defenses and create a much-needed attitude adjustment. Maybe your take on Scripture or interpretation of Biblical events causes someone to rethink their own spiritual positioning or re-evaluate their core faith beliefs. Perhaps your speaking up gives other Christians the courage and confidence to echo and affirm their beliefs in a hostile environment, too.

It's true that when you become the kind of impassioned advertiser God wants you to be and speak up with courage and conviction, there may be some spirited disagreement at times, even among your own family, Sunday school class or circle of friends. Assuming however, as I said, that everyone holds true to Biblical principles and teachings, I think varying opinions should be welcomed and embraced, whether you're among fellow worshippers in a Bible study or at a place away from your safety zone. Instead of getting angry and indignant over another's position, look at it as a chance to learn something from them. The opposing opinion they offer up may actually enlighten you and help you see certain Scripture passages in a new and different way. Some Christians thrive in situations where they can wrangle and debate spiritual issues with one another. Others don't. Either way, be receptive to Biblically grounded beliefs that may differ from your own. Who knows? God may be using them and their position to advertise to you!

## UP FOR DISCUSSION.

1. What things compete with your ability to pray and worship God? What things distract you from building a stronger relationship with Jesus Christ?

2. Why is it easier to trust in money more than God? If you poor, would you be more or less likely to respond to God and why?

3. God's love and grace is for everyone, but do you make assumptions about who you think is worthy to receive it? Does that make you more willing or more reluctant to advertise God to certain individuals or groups?

4. Why do we allow others to convince us we can't when God tells us we can?

5. God gives us a "voice." What situations tend to stifle yours? What events might cause you to speak up?

6. Spirited disagreement among Christians is normal and healthy. Under what conditions would you accept or reject another's arguments or beliefs?

# 8

## *Obstacles to Advertising God*

o o o o o o o o o o o o o o o o o o o o o o o o o o o o o o o o o

"I can do everything through Him who gives me strength."

—{ *Philippians 4:13* }

The word witness holds such a bad connotation in Christian circles. Say "witness" to churchgoers and watch how quickly their lips start to quiver and their bodies begin to tense up. You get the sense that a feeling of real panic is setting in. That's because, when it comes to witnessing, or advertising God, most Christians conjure up images of thumping a Bible on a crowded street corner or in front of a sports venue, parading up and down a city sidewalk wearing a sandwich board with a religious message on both sides, knocking on stranger's doors, or chasing down and badgering non-believers until they decide to accept Christ or an invitation to church.

But advertising God is so far removed from all those scenarios. As you've seen, advertising God doesn't have to be some pressure-packed, stress-filled event. It should be easy, genuine and oh by way, fun. Still, Christians experience major difficulties when it comes to advertising God. Some people cower in fear. Some have excessive pride. Some worry about offending another person or group. Some feel hypocritical for saying one thing and doing another. Some are unsure of their faith. Some cave in to social pressure. Some aren't confident they can provide Biblical back-up to support their beliefs. Some have priorities and ambitions that differ from God's. Some rationalize they just don't have the time to serve God. Some let apathy dictate their actions and inactions.

All of the above are common obstacles to advertising God and help comprise my list of the top ten reasons why Christians find it difficult to talk about God.

## 1. The Fear Factor

After hearing from and discussing the topic with many believers, fear is without a doubt one of the biggest impediments to advertising God and even perhaps the most common. Fear is something we all experience and it can manifest itself in so many different ways. You're scared you'll say or do the wrong thing. You're fearful of alienating yourself from friends and coworkers. You're frightened of the unknown and of the challenges and responsibilities your witness or volunteering might bring. Maybe you even have a fear of failure.

Fear seems to have a way of crippling you and making you do irrational things, and ultimately, it becomes the thing that flat out inhibits you from taking that initial step of faith or stops you dead in your tracks soon after you start. As a Christian, there comes a time when you must decide whether you will speak up and advertise God, or let your fears get the best of you and do nothing. President Franklin D. Roosevelt claimed, "The only thing we have to fear is fear itself." It was true after our nation was attacked in 1941 and it's true when we set off on a purpose-driven mission to serve and advertise God.

But fear itself is not necessarily a bad thing. Fear is a natural human emotion that helps protect you from danger. It's that little voice inside your head or a gut reaction that instinctively keeps you safe or prevents you from doing something foolish or reckless.

On the other hand, fear can also become your worst enemy. And because it is such a powerful emotion, fear is one of Satan's greatest weapons. After thousands of years of employing it in his arsenal, Satan knows all too well the impact of fear and how it can render Christians with the best intentions anxious, apprehensive and ineffective.

Fear isn't something many people want to acknowledge either because they don't want to be perceived as weak or cowardly. And because fear is so often internalized, it manifests itself through lame excuses and justifications. For example, in the church, it's quite common to hear phrases such as "I'm not sure I'm the right person to do that job," "I would love to do it, but..." "Maybe next time," or the old standby "I'm too busy." As I mentioned earlier, I always wonder how many opportunities God gives us to overcome our fears and step forward in faith before He moves on to someone else who's ready, willing and able to take up the task. Continue being the one who always gives in to your fears and you risk losing out on a great opportunity to be used by God. You don't want that kind of faith. You want the kind of faith that says "Yes, Lord, I'm fearful, but I'm more fearful of not doing what You ask of me, so I'm tossing my fears aside and trusting completely in You."

It's not easy to cast aside fear and grab hold of the promises of God. Maybe that's because your fear is sometimes a more powerful motivator than your faith. There's always some degree of apprehension or trepidation involved when you step out of your comfort space and take risks for Christ. Why do you think Peter denied Christ and all the disciples went into hiding after Christ's death? They were scared the same fate that had befallen Jesus awaited them. During this troubling time, I think their deep-seeded fear and apprehension made it extremely difficult for even the staunchest disciples to understand much less cling to the promises Christ made about His death and resurrection. We modern day disciples aren't too different now. Fear distracts us from fully believing in the promises of God and inhibits our ability to place our trust wholly in Him. When we let fear consume or overwhelm us, lots of times we do exactly what Jesus' disciples did—we go into hiding, letting our fears stymie the otherwise good things we could say and do for God.

## Go From Fearful to Faithful…Advertise God in any Situation

Rather than risk your social status, reputation and friendships, it's often easier to sit back and do nothing. And sadly, many are inclined to do just that. If you're not faithfully and passionately advertising God like you know you should, ask yourself what it is that keeps you from doing so. For many, fear of failure may the number one answer. Perhaps in part because from early childhood, we're taught to succeed in school, in sports, in a career, in marriage, in financial planning. Plus, we buy into all that success offers such as money, prestige, influence and respect. In a society that frowns upon failure, we're convinced there really is no such thing as a lovable loser.

Ted Williams is considered one of baseball's greatest and most prolific hitters. Yet only once in his illustrious career did he bat over .400 for an entire season, a feat that as of late 2006 has never been duplicated. In that exceptional season of 1941, "The Splendid Splinter", as great a hitter as he was, failed to get a base hit an amazing 60% of the time he went to the plate.

Still, no one considered Williams' batting average a failure. Instead, his batting average is hailed by fans, sportscasters and baseball purists as a remarkable individual achievement. By comparison, major league hitters today consider a good season one where they hit just .300. No one in the game considers them a failure either. In fact, these modern players are rewarded with multi-million dollar contracts despite the fact that even the best of them fail to get a hit a whopping 70% of the time they come up to bat. Imagine the consequences if you failed 70% of the time in your job!

In the game of life, even the best Christians can fail 70, 80 or 90% of the time they advertise God, but many of these same Christians remain undeterred, coming back again and again to take more swings for Christ. It's safe to say that every now and then you're going to strike out or get hit with a curveball when advertising God. And that's okay. So what do you do? You know the old saying—try, try again.

As we've seen, everyone just won't respond or react to the message you share, the money you need or the invitation you extend. Don't take it personally. It doesn't mean you are a failure when advertising God. It simply means, that for whatever reason, the person(s) to whom you're advertising God are unresponsive and unreceptive at this particular moment in time. Even the best motivational speakers in the world can't always sway people's attitudes or hold everyone's attention rapt. That's life. Remember, you're not a results-oriented Christian; you're a God-focused Christian.

Romans 8:31 tells us, "If God is for us, who can be against us?" Instead of sitting around the dugout and allowing fear of failure to rule your game, brush off the past, step confidently back into the batter's box, dig in your heels and swing for the fences. Just like the major leaguers, you're never going to bat 1.000, but if you're out there doing what God calls you to do, you are a full-fledged superstar in the eyes of God. Even if nothing happens or results aren't seen, God still won't see failure. You're a winner for getting in the game and doing all He asks of you. Leave the rest up to Him.

## Reject Rejection

Another thing that hinders our relationship with God is the fear of rejection. Most of us have a natural desire to please and to be liked and accepted among our family, friends and colleagues. Some can deal with rejection positively and move on, but for others, rejection is the ultimate humiliation and a devastating blow to their confidence and self-esteem.

One way to avoid rejection is by not saying or doing anything that would invite it. You know how it is. Keep things just the way they are and never do anything to rock the boat. After all, what would your friends, family or colleagues think if you suddenly expressed your religious views on God, faith and forgiveness? What would they say? What would they tell others about you behind your back? What if they alienated or ostracized you from the group?

Maybe these people are good friends, your girlfriend or boyfriend, your spouse, your child or your parent. In other words, they are people who are important to you. You know you need to share your faith and encourage them to get more involved in a relationship with God, but you fear they'll think you've gone "Christian" on them. What if they think you're not cool and no fun to hang out with anymore? What if they feel like all you do is preach to them? What if they think you no longer share the same beliefs and values as they do and they begin to drift away? What if they reject you and your message?

Yes, it's sometimes risky to advertise God, and it's entirely possible that valued friendships and cherished relationships could be jeopardized, especially if those with whom you once hung out with continue in lifestyles that go against God's teachings. But isn't it better that these earthly relationships are weakened or severed than endanger the one you have or want to establish with your heavenly Father?

What about you? Are you one who isn't about to chance things in order to keep your earthly relationships safe and intact? Or, are you one who will advertise God at all costs without fear of rejection or reprisal?

## Don't Let Satan's Scare Tactics Frighten You

The fears of failure and rejection are standard issue in Satan's weaponry. They are precisely the type of scare tactics he uses to quiet your tongue and stifle your will power to promote God. Satan's quite good at convincing you that it is easier to do nothing and maintain the status quo than it is to take a risk and advertise God. The reason is simple—he doesn't want you creating excitement for God's ways, chatting up His infinite love and goodness, or building enthusiasm and momentum for faith-based charity work or much-needed church projects.

Even if you're actively advertising God and doing His work, Satan still takes advantage of your fear and nervousness by trying to affect the outcome of the things you do for God. Don't think so? What about the lump in you get in your throat when you're asked to pray out loud in a Bible study group or Sunday school class? Or that churning in your stomach when your minister asks you to share your personal testimony with the congregation? Or the stress and anxiety you feel before singing a solo or performing in a church drama. These are the types of physical and mental manifestations Satan saddles you with in order to try and stop you from doing something positive for God.

It's no secret that Satan wants to intimidate you into silence. That's why he's planting seeds of doubt and failure in your mind all the time. Advertisers of God can't allow Satan to take advantage of their fears and insecurities and cultivate a defeatist mindset within. Learn to recognize Satan's ploys for what they really are—well-timed assaults aimed at preventing you from taking a leap of faith and pursuing duties and opportunities God has given you the honor and privilege of doing. Rather than feeling frightened and helpless, decisively reject the lies and deceit Satan lobs your way and redirect your focus on Christ and ask Him to help you overcome your fears. Of course, if you're not already advertising God out of a fear of rejection, Satan's not going to waste time bothering you. He's already got you right where he wants you—resigned to being rejected.

Keep in mind you are engaged in a real spiritual war here and Satan is a determined and formidable enemy. He's not about to just give up and surrender. Even though you may win a battle here and there, Satan promises to come back at a more opportune time to confuse and weaken you again. You must always be on guard for his salvos and sneak attacks, especially when you're feeling most vulnerable. The days when you're too busy, too tired or too apathetic to advertise God are just the kind of openings Satan watches and waits for to ensure your silence. It only takes one indecisive moment, one unspoken word or one missed opportunity on your part for Satan to claim victory. And why not? He may have just prevented you from sharing your faith, offering an encouraging prayer, or reaching out to someone who really needed it and who would have responded favorably to the message of Jesus Christ.

Yielding to fears rather than doing what God wants you to do ultimately paralyzes and prevents you from doing something you know you should. If you let fear control your actions, you let Satan win and God loses out on a chance to use you.

In reality, you should feel emboldened and empowered when Satan comes around threatening failure and rejection because he knows you're about to do something good for God. Instead of letting Satan scare you into doing nothing, turn the tables on him and use his lies and deceit as motivation to stand up for God in any circumstance.

Robert Louis Stevenson wrote, "Keep your fears to yourself, but share your inspiration with others." You never know how your words and deeds will impact others, so when the moment comes to advertise God, strap on the armor of Christ, fend off Satan's strikes, and boldly, proudly assert your Christian faith. Every time you share a simple prayer, acknowledge Jesus Christ as the leader of your life, extend an invite to church, or perform a service in His holy name, you make Satan a little weaker and your faith a little stronger by fearlessly professing your love and exhibiting an unwavering commitment to put the Lord first in spite of your misgivings.

## God Understands Your Fear

Thankfully, we worship a God who knows and understands our fears because He experienced them himself in man form. He can help you overcome your anxieties if you trust in Him completely, especially when your faith is really put to the test. It's understandable to have normal apprehension when you're trying something new or venturing into situations where it's not exactly comfortable or places where we feel oddly out of our element. But God doesn't send us out to fail—He sends us out to be the shining beacon of Christ in a sinful, ugly world. In 1 Peter 2:9, Peter asserts we "are a chosen people…a people belonging to God, that [we] may declare the praises of Him who called [us] out of the darkness into His wonderful light."

Ever noticed in a really scary horror movie that nothing bad ever happens when it's light outside, only when it's dark? It is the darkness that feeds our fears, stokes our imagination and drives our uneasiness. In the dark, there's danger, tension and apprehension. In the light, there's safety, security and clarity. Like a lighthouse beacon shining high above the craggy shoreline, Christ is the light of the world granting peace and calm to all who seek safe harbor in Him. Don't let fear inhibit your relationship with Christ. Confess and release your fears to God and take comfort in His promise in Psalm 91:14-15, "Because he loves Me, I will rescue him; I will protect him, for he acknowledges My name. He will call upon Me and I will answer him; I will be with him in trouble. I will deliver him and honor him."

## 2. You Feel Hypocritical

Be honest. How many times have you been in church worshiping on Sunday morning feeling so righteous and all full of the spirit, then you turn right around on the drive home and yell a not-so-spiritual obscenity at the lane-changer who rudely cut you off? Or realize you're knowingly active in the same sin you condemn others for. Or that you don't read the Bible, diligently pray or participate in a ministry like you tell others they should. It's easy to feel hypocritical at times because we all have weaknesses that leave us vulnerable and susceptible to sin.

Although Satan sees to it that the road to spiritual growth is fraught with pitfalls, we humans have more than enough fallacies, habits and tendencies that prevent us from sharing God's word day in and day out. Certainly all obedient Christians covet living a life that's pleasing to God, but we all fall short of our aspirations through sinful acts or by succumbing to our own fears and shortcomings. We make the wrong choices, we give in to temptations, we chum around with the wrong people, we justify bad actions with good excuses. All of which are in direct opposition to what God wants and desires for us to do.

And when we do commit sin, most Christians feel shame and remorse and immediately pray for God's forgiveness. But some sins are difficult to shake ourselves free from, and we find ourselves in a continual cycle of sinning and asking for forgiveness, sinning and asking for forgiveness over and over. Does that mean we are bad Christians or merely imperfect human beings with problems, habits and addictions that can't be dismissed in just a few days? I tend to think it's the latter. Good Christian people sometimes do bad things and earnestly seek repentance and God's forgiveness. It doesn't make us hypocritical—it makes us human. Fortunately, Jesus doesn't instruct others to be like us. He instructs us to be like Him.

## Sin is a Real Part of our Human Condition

We all struggle with sin and have weaknesses that make us feel and act hypocritical. It's part of our human condition, but you can't allow that fear of hypocrisy to stand in your way as you serve and honor God. The reality is, none of us is entirely sin-free. We're all going to mess up and do dumb things. Sometimes I imagine Christ shaking His head in disgust at all the sins we Christians collectively commit. Satan knows this too and he's quite good at playing on your conscience and convincing you that you are an undeserving candidate to serve God because of all those weak spots you have. But rather than yield to feelings of inadequacy and unworthiness, recall God's words to Paul in 2 Corinthians 12:9-10, "My grace is sufficient for you, for my power is made perfect in weakness." Take this verse to heart and like Paul, delight in your weakness, in your hardships, in your difficulties. For when you are weak, according to Paul, you are strong.

The reality is God knows what's truly in your heart and understands your struggle with sin. That's why he sent Jesus Christ to pardon us from the consequences of sin. As a Christian, it's also what makes you uniquely equipped to help others who wrestle with the same temptations and sinful indulgences you do. Instead of hiding behind your fear of hypocrisy, know that you have a wonderful opportunity to advertise God's redeeming love and forgiveness with someone who may be experiencing the same struggles and battling the same weaknesses as you.

*Advertising God in Real Life:*
*While sharing his testimony with the church congregation, Phillip confesses his addiction to drugs and alcohol and details the strain his dependencies have taken on*

*the relationships with his wife and children. He tells how, one day after being caught smoking pot in the house, his wife takes their kids and leaves him. The next day, she gives him an ultimatum—choose the drugs and alcohol or her and the kids. Phillip recalls hitting rock bottom after they left. Years of partying and irresponsibility had now cost everything near and dear to him. He tells how he felt emotionally and spiritually bankrupt and he wanted so very badly to change. He just didn't know how and he drank more to help him figure out a way. But instead of solace and answers, he only found despair.*

*Phillip's wife is an active member in the church and she always promised Phillip that God could help him cleanse himself of his addictions if only Phillip will ask. Feeling like he had nothing else to lose, Phillip emotionally describes how he went out into the backyard one night, fell to his knees in the cool, dew-covered grass and cried out for God to save him.*

*Confessing his sin and his need to have God occupy his heart, Phillip recounts how an immediate peace swept over him and how he felt the presence of God laying claim to him. It wasn't easy, but Phillip tells how he eventually kicked his habits and restored his relationship with his family. Now sober, Phillip regularly tells his story as he talks to and counsels others struggling with alcohol and drug dependencies.*

*Phillip advertises God by sharing his testimony, admitting his weaknesses and sins, and by passionately acknowledging how God can and will help others in similar situations.*

Like Paul, we can be made strong even when we're at our hypocritical worst and weakest. Whenever you're feeling dejected and discouraged by the hypocritical feelings sin often brings, remember that great prophets, priests, kings and disciples in the Bible were sinners just like you, yet God still used many of them to accomplish powerful and mighty things. When you sin, admit your mistake and pray for forgiveness, then get back out there and continue God's work. Challenge yourself to pursue the opportunities God lays out before you no matter what sinful "baggage" you carry around. Perhaps God has given you this very task to help you overcome the sins you feel so hypocritical about committing or to help another going through something you can relate to because you've been there yourself.

## 3. Flimsy Faith

Flimsy faith is another obstacle many Christians face when advertising God. Flimsy faith should not be confused with lack of faith. Rather, flimsy faith is faith that isn't strong or confident enough to endure or stand firm in all situations.

The writer of Hebrews 11:1 defines faith as "being sure of what we hope for and certain of what we do not see." Since there is no film footage of Christ's miracles, death and resurrection and none of us were there to witness or authenticate any of the Gospels firsthand, all Christians have some level of faith or they wouldn't be followers of Christ in the first place. Our acceptance of Christ is based on Scripture, the testimony of other believers and our own personal relationship and experiences with God.

Maybe there have been times when you wished for irrefutable proof that Christ really lived, died and rose again. But, if such evidence and documentation existed and you relied on it to support your spiritual beliefs, your faith would be rendered meaningless because you would likely put more trust in that which you could see rather than in the unseen things that are God.

In today's world, the media visually documents just about everything, so it takes genuine and steadfast faith to believe in an unseen God. To some degree, however, all of us are like the doubting disciple Thomas, to whom we give such a hard time. But truthfully, given the chance, wouldn't most of us want to see Jesus' nail-scarred hands and feet for ourselves in order to believe without a doubt in His triumph over death? I think we would.

## Faith Can Flatten Out at All Stages of Belief

Flimsy faith is something Christians of all ages and stages encounter over the course of their relationship with Christ. If you're a new Christian in the midst of a spiritual learning curve, faith is just beginning to take root and can be fleeting depending on the situation. You simply don't feel confident enough to share your testimony, participate in a spirited Sunday school lesson or volunteer to be on a committee or help out on a church mission project. You feel like you need more time to acclimate yourself to the teachings of Christ before committing to anything.

For maturing Christians, faith can remain delicate. You know the Word and try to live by Christ's example, but when trouble occurs, when you're challenged or belittled for following Christ's teachings instead of the world's, or when you're put in a position to speak up for your beliefs, your faith sometimes becomes introverted and you remain silent. You realize you need to strengthen your beliefs and become more passionate about sharing the message of Christ in all situations, but waffle between knowing what you ought to do for Christ and actually doing it on a consistent basis.

Long-time Christians aren't immune from the adverse affects of flimsy faith either. Although you're well-versed in Scripture and able to discern God's plan for you and confidently articulate your beliefs to others, faith can still stall out especially if you feel like you've taught or participated in every Sunday school class there is to teach, read and re-read the Bible, even taken every single Bible study or Christian enrichment course ever offered at your church. Faith stagnates because you feel like you've done it all and that there's nothing new for you to learn and experience. You want to be retooled and recharged as you look for new ways to encounter and serve God.

Everyone's faith process is different. Some are ready to put their faith into action right away while others need time and seasoning to become more effective at sharing and advertising the message of Christ. Regardless of where you are in your relationship with Christ, your faith will always remain tenuous unless it is spiritually nurtured, strengthened, energized and put to work to honor and glorify God.

## 4. You Like to Go with the Flow

Purposely or not, many Christians find that it's sometimes easier to blend in than stand out. It's understandable. Being the one out front leaves many of us feeling vulnerable to ridicule, criticism and failure. Rather than speak confidently as a follower of Jesus Christ, some find that it's much easier, much safer and much more politically correct to stay in the shadows instead of challenging and discussing the anti-Christian beliefs and opinions of others or questioning the accepted, but outdated, practices of some churches or religious institutions. But blending in is not something Christians should aspire to do or even want to do. Paul writes in Romans 12:2 that you are not to "conform any longer to the pattern of this world, but be transformed by the renewing of your mind."

In my line of work, I experience feelings of conformity on a regular basis. When meeting or dining with clients, I always try to avoid controversial social issues, politics, child rearing and any other topic that opens the way for impassioned, opinionated discussion. Occasionally, however, the topic of religion will come up. Most of the time the talk is tame and generic, but sometimes a colleague or client will make a negative or insulting remark about God, the church or Christian beliefs in general that I feel warrants a response. Being in a service-oriented business, this frequently puts me in a conflicted position. On the one hand, I'm a paid contractor and they are my client, so I feel the need to nod in a noncommittal way, neither approving nor disapproving, and try as quickly as possible to steer the conversation towards a less inflammatory subject. On the other, I am a follower and servant of Jesus Christ and feel equally compelled to come to the defense of God. It's a tough position to be in as a hired hand, but as

I've steadily grown more comfortable advertising God, I find I can make a short positive statement about my own faith without condoning or belittling the other person's beliefs.

I'm reminded again of Galatians 1:10. Are we trying to please people or Christ? If we're trying to please and appease people, Paul tells us we're not being a faithful servant of Christ. I feel that if it's okay for others to speak their opinion, they should respect me for sharing mine, even if the two ideas are in conflict. If you've found yourself in a similar situation, maybe you've also discovered as I have that there's usually someone else at the table or in the group who was glad you spoke up and voiced your beliefs. Your courage and conviction could very well influence that other person to be the one who speaks up first the next time.

One particular event where I mistakenly went with the flow has bothered me for over ten years. At a business dinner one night, I was seated at the far end of a long table with several colleagues and clients. Appetizers and drinks snaked across our table, which was situated just beside a doorway that led out onto the city sidewalk. As we talked, a homeless woman suddenly entered the restaurant and made her way towards the opposite end of the table from me. She asked two of my coworkers seated nearest the door for food and money. Annoyed, both men impatiently waved her away. Undaunted, the woman continued to the next person, then the next, each time receiving the same irritated look and shooing of the hand. As she moved closer to me, I reached inside my wallet and discreetly tucked twenty dollars in my palm. Suddenly, I began to grow more concerned about the chiding I'd get from the others rather than the spiritual joy I would get by helping this woman so I stuffed the bill back in my pocket. When the homeless woman finally approached and asked if I could help, I politely smiled and shook my head no. Dejected, she turned and walked out of the restaurant. No one had offered her so much as a single dime. All of us that night were guilty of viewing the woman with disdain instead of pity, with annoyance instead of compassion.

As she turned to leave, the look of genuine disappointment registered in the woman's eyes touched me deeply, and in the moment it took for her to get out the door, I decided to follow my initial instinct and give her the money regardless of what anyone said or thought. I quickly excused myself and headed out the door. Although I was behind her by less than a minute, the woman had simply vanished by the time I reached the sidewalk. My eyes darted up and down the street for any sign of her, but she had disappeared as quickly and mysteriously as she had first appeared.

I was ashamed of myself that day for several reasons, but mostly because I chose the approval of others over the approval of God. I also knew that had I done the right thing and offered the homeless woman money in the name of Christ, others may well have reconsidered and chipped in a few bucks, too. Any of us at the table that night could have advertised God by showing Christ-like compassion to the woman. Instead of going with the flow and caving in to peer pressure, I wish I had been the one to step forward and offer her the money as testimony to my love of Jesus Christ.

I don't know that twenty dollars would have made much difference in the homeless woman's life, but I do know I could have let others that night see the light of Christ burning in me. God gave me a chance to do that and I let Him down by allowing the callous actions of others to influence me instead of allowing God to work through me. As similar situations have come up, I always remember the feeling of disappointment and regret God left with me that night. Now, I try to follow the loving example of Christ instead of joining in with the indifference of others.

## You Can't Please All the People All the Time

As a dedicated Christian, you're not here to win a popularity contest. You're here to spread the gospel of Jesus Christ, not by going with the flow, but by going against the grain and following the loving approach set forth by our Lord. Regrettably, some people will not like what you say or do. Likewise, they may not even like you because of what you say and what you do. Pharaoh didn't like it when Moses told him to set the Israelites free. King David "burned with anger" when he was rebuked by the prophet Nathan for sleeping with Bathsheba and having her husband Uriah murdered. Ahab sulked and seethed when Elijah confronted him about stealing Naboth's vineyard. The Pharisees plotted to kill Jesus when Jesus proclaimed He was indeed the Son of God.

In my industry where creativity is so subjective, I find myself using the phrase "you can't please all the people all the time" quite a lot. It's one of those classic Mom-isms you always heard as a child, but it's true—you can't always be a people-pleaser. You can be the very best at what you do, but there will always be at least one person out there who isn't happy with what you say or your Christ first approach to life. It's impractical and naive to believe otherwise. Even Nordstrom, a prominent national retailer renowned for offering superior customer service, fails to please every single customer on every single visit.

The point I'm making is that you can't allow the fear of disapproval stop you from experiencing the joys of advertising God. You can control what you say and do, but you can't totally control how people react to it. Some will commend your actions, others are bound to criticize them. But, whether you are praised or condemned when advertising God, take heart in the fact that you didn't go with the flow. You stood up for the Lord and did what Christians are supposed to do—let others see the love of Jesus Christ in you. Do this and God will surely be well pleased.

## 5. Lack of Confidence and Biblical Knowledge

As disciples of Christ, we are called to immerse ourselves in God's word, not infrequently as so many of us are inclined to do, but every single day. You make time to read books and magazines, watch TV, play video games, and surf the Internet, but, other than Sunday mornings, how often do you actually pick up the Bible and read it? St. Bernard of Clairvaux said, "The person who thirsts for God eagerly studies and meditates on the inspired Word."[10]

What may surprise you is just how little time even the thirstiest of Christians spend reading his or her Bible and reflecting on God's word. One statistic I came across is astonishing. An impressive 92% of Americans admitted to owning a Bible[11], but according to Barna Research, only 47% will read it weekly outside of church.[12] Because of all of life's daily distractions, many Christians only quench their thirst for Scripture at church and never satisfy their real need, which is to read and study the Bible for themselves independent from worship or a structured Bible study. Christians who want to maximize their potential and advertise God to the fullest must learn to make Bible reading and prayer a daily habit rather than occasional indulgence. A news radio station in Atlanta once used the slogan "If you miss a day, you miss a lot." The same can be said when you skip reading the Bible. You definitely miss out on the spiritual nourishment you need to survive and thrive every day.

Reading the Bible is essential for all Christians. Still, meaningful time spent with the Bible is something many Christians readily admit they could improve upon. Many believers make resolutions every new year to read the Bible with greater regularity, but like most resolutions, good intentions give way to old habits after only a few months, especially when they encounter a book that's difficult to read and interpret or when they are troubled because they don't understand the meaning, relevance or imagery of particular passages.

Sanctioned by God, the Bible is the ultimate authority on all spiritual matters. It is God's voice passed along by man in written form to give Christians spirit-breathed guidelines and instruction for healthy, faith-based living and servitude. The Bible speaks to us in so many wonderful ways, and as Christians intent on advertising God, we need to discipline ourselves to read and know Scripture, apply it to our lives and be able to communicate its message to others. We all have our favorite verses, but part of advertising God is knowing which books, chapters and verses speak to the person or target market with whom you're addressing. Committing yourself to learning and studying the Bible not only gives you confidence to share His word, but also breeds familiarity with all 66 books so you can find the verses that add validity and support to your words and beliefs. Knowing the Bible also helps you locate verses that can be meaningful and beneficial to others as well.

Unlike the latest bestseller you read once and where the outcome is always the same, the Bible enlightens you in new and exciting ways every time you read it. No matter how many times you've read a particular book, chapter or specific verse, the Bible has the power to affect you on so many different levels depending on the state of mind you're in when you read it. Passages you've read dozens of times before can take on amazing new meaning. Verses you've previously skimmed right over and never connected with suddenly speak to you with new-found relevance. Stories that once seemed insignificant become inspiring and empowering upon a second reading.

Several years back, I participated in a 32-week Bible study that required I read about 75% of the Bible, including a large portion of the Old Testament. That first time reading through, I highlighted hundreds of great passages for future reference. My Bible looked like a sea of yellow lines. The next year, I participated in the second of these series and though it was suggested we use a new Bible, I chose to use the Bible I had from the first year. Some readings were the same as the previous year, and I was amazed at just how many of the verses I did not underline the first time I read them. Upon a second reading, many of these same verses spoke to me in a way they hadn't when I initially read them.

All of which proves you can't just read the Bible once and be done with it. Though you may have read the stories and inspirational verses again and again, God's Scripture continues to offer you an infinite array of life-sustaining guidance, directives and affirmations that help you grow in your faith. Think about Psalm 23 or John 3:16. You probably memorized these beloved verses as a child, but you still find comfort and peace in them even after hundreds of readings and recitations.

Many ministers will tell you one of the main reasons why Christians don't read the Bible as much as they should is a perceived lack of time. With school, long commute times, family and recreational obligations, household chores and work responsibilities, many of us find it difficult to squeeze in time to do much of anything, let alone read the Bible. Sure, our intentions are good, but when time constraints cause us to fall behind schedule, we have to make sacrifices and reading the Bible is something that's often very easy to neglect. And even when time is available, it seems we usually find it easier to watch TV, pick up a magazine or play video games rather than dive into a sustained Bible reading.

Let's face it, we make time to eat and sleep, shave and shower, exercise and work out. Isn't reading the Bible just as important to our daily well-being and overall happiness? Don't let Satan convince you that you don't have an extra 30 minutes a day to read the Bible. Get up a few minutes earlier or go to bed a little later. Designate a specific time and place at home where you're not to be disturbed. Take your Bible to work and read on your lunch hour (it's a great way to advertise God to your colleagues and you'd be surprised how many of them will notice a Bible on your bookshelf or credenza). Read your Bible on the commuter train or bus instead of skimming the newspaper or a magazine. Saving time is like saving money. You'll be surprised just how quickly it adds up when you do the simplest things.

For those who struggle with Bible deficiency, here are a few helpful and proven strategies that can help get you back on track reading your Bible with greater regularity and enthusiasm. First, like starting a diet or exercise program, you must make a realistic commitment to read the Bible on a daily basis and stick to it no matter what. Choose a time during the day when you are alert and can read, reflect and enjoy quiet time with God without distractions or interruptions. Maybe it's early in the morning before everyone else is awake, during your lunch hour at work or right after dinner. To find more privacy, you may have to read in bed, as you soak in the bath or sneak down to the basement. Just find the time and place that works best for you and don't set unreasonable goals. Read for 15 minutes, a half hour or as long you're able. Find a Bible you like and a translation you can understand. Choose a Bible that's easy to read with a typeface that won't strain your eyes. For added clarification and insight, choose a study Bible with notes that help you better comprehend and apply the Scriptures you're reading. Become familiar with your Bible and the order of all 66 books so you can quickly identify, locate and cross-reference verses. As you read, make notes in a journal or in the margins of your Bible. Use different color highlighter pens to underline verses that have special meaning to you, then memorize them or create a color key for your highlighted marks so you can readily share those passages when you advertise God.

Moreover, many Christians find they can really benefit from some type of structured reading program whether it's a daily devotional, independent study or being part of a small class or group. If your church doesn't offer a regular Bible study or share group, be proactive. Starting or sponsoring a Bible study is another good way to advertise God. If you're interested in finding other Bible reading solutions on your own, type in the phrase "reading the Bible" on any Internet search engine and you'll find countless online programs, books and suggestions with such titles as One Year Bible Reading Plan, Daily Bible Readings, How to Read the Bible, Why Read the Bible, Interactive Bible Study, and many more. You're just a point and click away from thousands of great ideas!

Another reason ministers cite for poor Bible reading skills is that many people aren't exactly sure where to start reading. Do you start with Genesis and keep going in book order, begin with the New Testament, follow a devotional reading plan found in your Bible or on the Internet, or just open up your Bible and start reading wherever your eyes happen to land? My advice—start wherever you want and take it from there. In my opinion, as long as you're reading your Bible, it doesn't really matter which Testament, which book or which verse you start with.

Over the years, I've also discovered that, with the exception of Genesis and the Psalms, lots of Christians avoid or entirely dismiss reading the Old Testament altogether. I think they consider Old Testament books mere recordings of Jewish history and a detailed litany of antiquated covenant laws. That's part of its story to be sure, but if you're not reading the 39 books of the Old Testament, you're missing out on nearly 60% of God's holy and unfailing word. Aside from all the great stories you may have loved as a child like Samson and Delilah, David and Goliath, and Daniel in the lion's den, the Old Testament is filled with applicable instruction for advertising God. Just take a look at Deuteronomy 5:32-33 and 6:5. Ponder Job 11:13-15. Or contemplate what Proverbs 3:5-6 and 16:3 has to say. Read Isaiah 7:9, 41:9-10 and 58:11. Flip to Ezekiel 18:27-28 or 33:8-9. Thumb to Joel 2:32 and Micah 6:8. Find Habakkuk 3:18. Don't let the "old" in Old Testament fool you. The messages and teachings found there are as timeless and current today as they were thousands of years ago. Overlooking these pearls of Godly wisdom or failing to share them with others handicaps you in your ability to advertise God.

Paul writes in 2 Timothy 3:16-17 that "all Scripture is God-breathed and is useful for teaching, rebuking, correcting and training in righteousness, so that the man of God may be thoroughly equipped for every good work." Consistently reading the Bible allows you to feed and nourish your spiritual appetite, grow your faith and develop a stronger relationship with Jesus Christ, get direct and supreme guidance from God, defend yourself when fighting temptation, and gain confidence to find and quote relevant Scripture when you need it.

Rather than come up some catchy closing that really drives home the point of reading your Bible every day, I think I'll borrow the words of Saint Isidore. He says, "Prayer purifies us, reading instructs us. If a man wants to be always in God's company, he must pray regularly and read regularly. When we pray, we talk to God; when we read, God talks to us. All spiritual growth comes from reading and reflection. By reading we learn what we did not know; by reflection we retain what we have learned. Reading the Holy Scriptures confers two benefits. It trains the mind to understand them; it turns man's attention from the follies of the world and leads him to the love of God."[13]

Make Bible reading a daily commitment and you'll discover newfound joy and peace in God and also be equipped with the spiritual knowledge you need to become more a confident advertiser of God.

## 6. Apathy

Apathy is what I like to call the "let-someone-else-do-it" syndrome and it ranks right up there as one of the single biggest problems when it comes to advertising God. It's not that Christians don't care about reaching out to others. Many Christians just don't want to be the ones reaching out, especially when the action of reaching out takes them away from their comfort zone or the safety of familiar surroundings. If you're a church leader, project coordinator, Sunday School teacher or committee chairperson searching for able and willing volunteers, you've undoubtedly run into this type of apathy many times before and know exactly what I am talking about.

Maybe you know someone who has an apathetic attitude. Maybe it's you. Regrettably, far too many Christians are quite content to go to church on Sunday mornings, sing, pray and worship for an hour or so, and then go on with their lives until the next Sunday. My brothers and I had this toy racetrack we loved to play with as kids. What made that racetrack so cool was that, just as the two cars began to slow down at the end of each lap, they would pass through this spinning device that would rev the cars up, then shoot them out the other side in a burst of speed enabling the cars to race on for another lap. This cycle would continue as long as we let the cars race.

The mindset of the once-a-week Christian reminds me of that nifty little racetrack. The once-a-week Christian gets all revved up after Sunday morning's service, but by the next Saturday, they begin to wind down and must be re-energized again for the following Sunday morning. They live out their Christian life week to week rather than moment to moment. And although the once-a-week Christian can be very loving, tithe generously and adhere to strong faith values, they tend to turn a blind eye to all the work that needs to be done in the church's ministry and outreach programs by only participating on Sunday mornings. They rationalize church work or mission projects always seem to get done and someone else will always step forward to do it. The once-a-week Christian has no genuine inclination to get involved and convinces himself that he doesn't have the time and that there are plenty of people much better equipped to answer the call than him. Regardless of all the excuses or justifications he can muster, it's really Christian complacency at its very worst.

What if Jesus and His disciples would have taken this kind of apathetic mind set? Some crowds would have never heard Jesus' teachings. Some of the lame and diseased would have never been healed. Countless churches would have never been started. If you're that once-a-week Christian, don't kid yourself. God needs you on a full-time faith basis. Your church needs you. Your fellow Christians need you. Those needing to be served need you.

You may think all the work gets done, but in reality it always doesn't. Many churches experience a dearth of volunteerism. When it comes to church members doing God's work, the old adage that 90% of the work is done by 10% of the people seems to ring true. All too frequently, it's the dedicated few time after time who sign up to do most of the work. Unfortunately fatigue, burn out and time restraints limit all the good things they can do and the places they can go. Since usually only a precious few will step forward to volunteer or administer the work, the church simply cannot live up to its Godly obligations and people who would benefit from the love and generosity of the church often go without the money, food, companionship or services they need.

God bless the myriad of selfless volunteers in today's churches for their tireless energy, enthusiasm and commitment. They are the ones who do the lion's share of the work and cheerfully do whatever task is asked of them. They are the bedrock of Christ and the church needs more people like them. Unfortunately, many of these people may not be the best match for certain projects because the spiritual gifts they possess aren't being properly channeled into areas that would be of maximum benefit to God and those they are serving. It's like the kicker on a football team forced to become linebacker because nobody else wants the job. It's just not the best fit and creates conditions that are ripe for failure.

Today's churches have a lot of "kickers" and not near enough "linebackers." It doesn't have to be this way, nor should it be if your faith is in the right place. It's similar to tithing. If everyone in the church cheerfully and faithfully gave their fair share through regular tithing, church coffers would be overflowing, and the sight of a wearied financial chairperson standing before the congregation pleading for money year in and year out would be a sight likely never seen again. Likewise, if every member of the local church was actively involved in one or more of its ministries, outreach programs and service projects or found ways to effectively advertise God through words, music, art, drama and teaching, just imagine how many people would be drawn to and affected by the loving grace of Jesus Christ. Pews every Sunday would be filled to capacity! This is how it should be when Christians have their priorities in harmony with God.

## It's Your Task to Do

In British Prime Minister Tony Blair's address to the U.S. Congress in July 2003, when referencing the war on terrorism, he addressed the apathy and complacency of people in a way that I believe applies to those who skew towards apathy rather than consistently seek to further the will of God. Blair said, "I know out there is a guy getting on with his life, perfectly happy, minding his own business, saying to you the political leaders of this country, 'Why me? Why us? Why America?' And the only answer is because destiny put you in this place in history, in this moment in time, and the task is yours to do."[14]

Now substitute a few choice words and read how Blair's message takes on new meaning in a way I believe is applicable to apathetic Christians. "I know out there is a guy getting on with his life, perfectly happy, minding his own business, saying to you the church leaders, 'Why me? Why us? Why our church?' And the only answer is because destiny put you in this place in history, in this moment in time, and the task is yours to do."

Spreading the word and love of Jesus Christ as He instructs in the Great Commission truly is our task to do. We Christians can't shirk our responsibilities by rationalizing that a project or a need is the task of that guy or that group to do. We must seize ownership and make it our duty. It is God's purpose for each of us to do all we can to help bring others to Christ with whatever resources and talents are made available to us.

Assuming someone else will always step forward and do things that need to be done is spiritual laziness and an impediment to advertising God. God doesn't need any more apathetic or un-revved, once-a-week Christians on His team. He's got plenty of those. Instead of leaving the work for all the others to do, God needs believers like you to boldly and courageously step forward and take advantage of the spiritual gifts He's given you so you can become an influential team player that helps win souls for God. In the church community, there is a real need to move more Christians from the confines of complacency into prolific participation.

## We Advertise God by Doing the Work He Commands

Advertising God is more than just words and promises. People also see God in you based on your actions and the Godly acts you perform. For example, you can tell someone as a nice gesture that you'll pray for them. But it becomes more meaningful and impactful, when you take their hand and pray for or with them right there on the spot. Some will also throw money at things and feel like they've made a significant contribution. And while donating money is a good and worthwhile thing, there's nothing like giving up time on the weekend to do some "sweat equity" in the name of the Lord. Visible, tangible actions like this have a profound and lingering affect on others because it gives them a chance to feel the presence and power of our living God and demonstrates a caring and compassionate commitment to the way you live out your faith.

Rather than keep your faith to yourself, share it with the community around you. If you see a need, address it. If you see an opportunity, seize it. If you feel a call, answer it. If you see work that needs done, volunteer. Advertising God is not about internalizing your faith. Christians cannot be introverts. Advertising God is all about getting out of your comfort zone and pursuing the God-directed duties and challenges you agreed to take on the moment you accepted Christ as your Lord and Savior.

And being a Godly witness is one task every Christian is called to do. God wants us to bear fruit, not sit on our hands and wither on the vine. Recalling Prime Minister Tony Blair's speech, now is our moment in time to discover what we as individual Christians do best—seek out opportunities to advertise God, and put our talent to work to faithfully and successfully execute God's will wherever and whenever that may be.

Don't let anyone convince you that you are without a talent. As we saw in Chapter 5, all of us, regardless of age, race, education, income or stature, have some God-given gift that's just waiting to be put to use. We see people all the time who have obvious spiritual gifts, but for one reason or another, fail to acknowledge or utilize these gifts for the glory of God. Ministers and active lay people alike agree that it's frustrating to see such talent go to waste especially when there's so much work to be done for God's kingdom. God gives each of us the tools. God gives us the resources. God gives us the energy and motivation. God gives us the power to do wonderful and mighty things. Things that didn't seem possible for you are now made possible when you genuinely give over your entire self to God.

Does that mean advertising God will always be easy, comfortable and convenient? Absolutely not! God never promised that it would be, and you shouldn't expect or demand it to be that way either. Besides, if following and advertising God were easy, comfortable and convenient, doing His work would not be an exercise in love, sacrifice and faith.

## 7. Pride

Pride is yet another reason some fail to advertise God to their fullest potential. Whether it's arrogance, selfishness or just downright stubbornness, many people frequently fail to convey the humility Christ teaches in the New Testament. Maybe you're one who is more concerned about your image or what others think of you. Maybe you're one who doesn't like getting involved in the "grunt" work mission outreach or servitude often requires. For instance, some feel like they're above working in a dingy soup kitchen, assisting needy families, painting church walls or pulling weeds at the local shelter. If this sounds like you, your attitude is all wrong. These are precisely the kinds of deeds Christ teaches His followers to do, working and ministering to the least and the lost. Without the ability to humble yourself before others and before God, you can't be the good and faithful servant Christ wants you to be.

Pride also manifests itself in Christians who feel they are more worthy of God's love, blessings and attention than others who haven't accepted Christ or who are of a lower social or economic status. Which again is just plain wrong. God certainly doesn't love some people more than others. In fact, Peter tells us in Acts 2:21 that "everyone who calls on the name of the Lord will be saved." That means Jews and Gentiles, Protestants and Catholics, rich and poor, criminals and addicts, the smart and the not-so-smart. Faith-focused Christians sincerely committed to following Christ's teachings should make a concerted effort to become more humble, less self-centered and even less judgmental. Misguided Christians who can't do these three things miss one of the main points in Christ's teachings—love one another as Jesus himself loves us. People who elevate themselves or their needs above others become like the guests Jesus criticized for seeking the best seats in the parable of the wedding feast in Luke 14:7-11. They want to be honored and glorified without being humbled, not humbled so they can be honored and glorified in Christ's kingdom.

The writer of Proverbs reminds us in 11:2 that, "When pride comes, then comes disgrace, but with humility comes wisdom." Pride can get us into all sorts of trouble when we let it displace our obedience to God. Dennis, a young associate pastor of a church I belonged to as a young adult shamefully shared this story with the congregation. As Dennis was locking up the front door of the church after working late one Friday night, a man stepped out of a shadowy recess and startled him. Fearful of being assaulted and robbed, Dennis tugged at the door trying to duck back inside the church. But with the door already locked, Dennis had no choice but to turn around, see what the man wanted and hope for the best.

As the man stepped into the light, Dennis could see his clothes were rumpled and his face haggard and unshaven. Physically intimidating this man was not. Dennis described him as being in his mid-thirties, short and lean with the strong scent of whiskey and cigarettes fouling his breath. Dennis saw the man's car parked in the lot, a faded red sedan with missing hubcaps and a cracked windshield. Dennis assumed the man was an alcoholic, living in his car and had come to the church in search of a handout.

Dennis admitted bristling at the thought of giving this man any money from either his own wallet or that of the church's discretionary fund used to help those really in need, not some down-on-his-luck drunk like this guy. Angry and indignant, Dennis figured the man would only use it to buy more booze and smokes and would be back again in a few days looking for even more cash. Dennis recalled chastising him and callously sending the man away empty handed. Instead of finding the compassion he sought and expected to find at the church, the man received nothing but contempt.

When God laid that sinful mistake on Dennis' heart the next day, Dennis began to understand how wrong his reaction had been to the man. Dennis had made hasty assumptions about him, immediately deeming the man unworthy of monetary help and of God's love. After sharing his story, Dennis confessed to having let his pride and selfishness govern his actions rather than abiding by the teachings of Jesus Christ. As a human being, Dennis was sorry for turning the man away. As a minister, he expressed shame and regret for not spending more time with him trying to get to the root of what his real needs were, physically and spiritually. Maybe Dennis could have helped him find a job, get into AA and locate a warm, safe place to stay. He could have invited him back to church, helped get him into counseling, asked if the man had any family. Looking back, Dennis realized he could have done a lot of things differently that night and been a more loving representative of God than he was.

Can you see a little bit of Dennis in yourself? Like Dennis, we sometimes let our pride get in the way of the things God teaches us to do, only to regret it later because we know we missed an important opportunity to advertise God and show love to another. When you come to Christ, you have to let your pride go by the wayside so you can serve God no matter what He asks you to do. Mother Teresa referred to this as being "covered with the poverty of the Cross, covered with the obedience of the Cross, and covered with the charity of the Cross."[15] It's the ability to cloak yourself in the mindset of Jesus Christ, forsake the "me-first" attitude the world teaches and discover the rewards of having a humble and charitable heart that beats strongly and loudly for the Lord.

## 8. We Put Conditions and Limits on God

We humans are a pretty smart bunch, but regardless of our vast intelligence, we can never fully fathom the extraordinary love and infinite abilities of God. It's not our fault. God is far too big and magnificent for mere mortals to totally comprehend His supreme greatness while we're here on earth.

I'm always amazed at believers and non-believers alike who, through their own misconceptions and misunderstandings, try to qualify or put restrictions on all the things God can and cannot do. According to Matthew 19:26, all things are possible with God. Pay attention to the wording here. The Bible doesn't say some things or a few things are possible, it says all things. Don't you think the God who created the heavens, the earth and the tiniest microscopic life, the God who developed the intricate workings of nature, the God who miraculously heals, and the God who triumphed over death can do anything He wants, anytime He wants? You simply cannot put limitations on God because God cannot be bound by human constrictions or the earthly boundaries of time, place and space. Satan, however, will try his hardest to convince you otherwise, especially in situations where things seem bleak, hopeless or seemingly beyond your ability to enact change.

In 1 Corinthians 3:19 Paul proclaims, "The wisdom of this world is foolishness in God's sight." No matter how brainy you are, when you accept Jesus Christ as your personal savior, you can't allow your human intellect or that of others to discount or quantify God's supreme authority even if such things fly in the face of the laws of nature, science and sensible reason. I believe this kind of thinking comes about because too many Christians are guilty of saying to themselves, "If I can't do it, neither can God." Or they assume, and wrongly so, that the very nature of their request is just too big for God to handle. Like when a loved one or friend is in an irreversible coma, or survival defies all logical odds, or brokering permanent peace between war-mongering nations. That "can't do" attitude is Satan talking. Learn to recognize it and don't allow the taunts of the enemy to weaken your steadfast belief in God's awesome power.

As a Christian, believe wholeheartedly in the unbelievable and in the possibility of the impossible even when all the doubters and naysayers claim it can't be done. Any limitations you or someone else imposes on God underscore an abject failure to fully acknowledge who God is and a reluctance to accept all the things He is quite capable of doing. When you pigeonhole God to fit your own preconceived notions and expectations, it's like snubbing your nose at His Almighty authority. And, just as positive declarations about God are quite contagious, this kind of rampant negativity equally rubs off on others, only in a bad way.

Some things God does will absolutely defy explanation and simply won't make any rational sense to anyone, even Christian believers who pray for and fully expect miracles. You don't have to understand why or how God does something though. What you do need to do however is embrace such miracles and success stories when you see, hear or experience them first hand, then use those happenings to advertise the glorious power of Almighty God. After all, did it make sense that the Red Sea could part, allowing the Israelites to travel safely through on dry ground? Did it make sense a man could walk on water or quiet a raging storm? Did it make sense that thousands of people would be fed from five loaves of bread and two small fish? Did it make sense that men could be raised from the dead? Did it make sense to walk around thick city walls, blow a trumpet and have the walls come crashing down? Of course not! But that's because we look at such events from a limited human perspective, not God's limitless perspective.

When we break free of our preconceived notions about what God can and cannot do, we start to see Him for who He really is and learn to faithfully believe in and accept all the mighty and wonderful things He is able to accomplish.

My grandfather once had the Scripture verse from Mark 11:24 taped prominently on his desktop at work. It reads, "Therefore, I tell you, whatever you ask for in prayer, believe that you have received it, and it will be yours." I was always struck by the authority of that passage and of the awesomeness of God's supreme majesty it portrays. When read in conjunction with Luke 17:6 where Jesus talks about having just a little faith when you ask for something (even faith the size of teeny-tiny mustard seed!), Mark's passage becomes even stronger and underscores the prodigious ability of our Lord to get things done, even the things that are seemingly impossible or against all odds. But remember Matthew 19:26—all things are possible with God! Believe it, embrace it, and take advantage of it in your life.

## 9. The Devil Makes You Not Do It

If I asked you to conjure up an image of Satan, you'd probably picture a heinous, despicable demon, the ugliest, most hideous and scariest-looking creature you've ever laid eyes on. Or would the traditional horned guy in the flaming red suit with forked tail and pitchfork come to mind? I don't think either of these descriptions accurately paints a true portrait of who Satan is. Rather than being the gory Hollywood stereotypes, I envision Satan being a particularly attractive entity, one who is in all likelihood charming, beguiling, likable and engaging. Yet beneath his appealing facade, Satan is brilliantly cunning and dangerously deceiving. He is the quintessential wolf in sheep's clothing. Why do you think the Internet porn business is booming, recreational drug use is so rampant and sex outside marriage is so common? The titillation, the highs, the money, the sheer excitement—it all seems so innocent, so attractive, so enticing.

You shouldn't be surprised that there are negative forces and bad influences out there opposing your best intentions to advertise God. The main competitor for Christian believers is Satan and he thrives on spiritual apathy, weakness and laziness. Peter describes Satan as an enemy who prowls around like a lion looking for someone to devour. As God's archenemy, Satan is your chief adversary and will do anything and everything he can to destroy, disrupt, discredit and otherwise thwart your plans and efforts to advertise God.

Clever and crafty, ruthless and unrelenting, damaging and detrimental, Satan is the very antithesis of God. God disapproves of and forgives sin; Satan flagrantly encourages and condones sin. God gives life, Satan takes it. God is a friend to the righteous, Satan a companion of the wicked. God blesses, Satan destroys.

Like companies that compete for your business, Satan is constantly trying to lure you away from God with a daily assault of tempting offers that are often very hard to pass up, even for staunch and faithful Christian believers. Like a skilled market researcher or telemarketer following a sales script, Satan knows exactly which strategies work on you and the ones that don't. He knows which buttons to push and which emotions to trigger. And if you successfully fend him off one day, he'll be back the next, undaunted and eager to try again.

Don't put the blinders on. You are engaged in a real spiritual dogfight here, constantly battling the lies and deceit Satan uses to pull you away from a life geared towards God. Let your guard down even once and Satan will be there to exploit it. Jesus knew this when He warned the disciples in Mark 14:38 to, "Watch and pray so that you will not fall into temptation. The spirit is willing but the body is weak."

Satan reminds me of the evil cyborg played by actor Robert Patrick in the popular *Terminator 2* film that was sent to destroy, or terminate, Arnold Schwarzenegger's character. Programmed to successfully complete his mission at all costs, Patrick's cyborg is majorly undeterred. He never aborts, never stops and constantly reinvents himself, adapting into any setting so he can gain the advantage.

I think it's the same way with Satan. Nothing Satan does, nor the depths to which he will sink should surprise you. As the enemy of salvation, he's been doing these things since the dawn of time and has a destructive track record littered with empty promises and broken souls to prove it. You can't completely stop him on your own because sin is inevitable in life, but you can deter him by following the instruction in Ephesians 6:11 where Paul implores you to, "Put on the full armor of God so that you can take your stand against the devil's schemes." The good news in all of this is that Satan couldn't ruin God's plan for the new covenant by keeping Christ in the grave, and one day Satan will be permanently defeated and forever vanquished by God. That's actually great news we should be out there emphasizing to all battle-weary Christians and those who want to reach up to Christ but are mired in Satan's sinful grip.

Until the ultimate day of defeat comes however, you must learn how to stand against Satan's schemes by strengthening your own spiritual focus. That involves prayer, Bible reading, church and mission involvement and getting past all the obstacles to advertising God we've talked about in this chapter. Because he is allowed by God to roam unfettered on earth, we must always be ready to defend ourselves from Satan's advances. Picture it this way. While you're trying so hard to live a life that's pleasing and beneficial to God, it is Satan who is gleefully snatching at your heels hoping to pull you back down into the pit of sin and worldly desire. And it's here he aims to keep you so he can prevent and disinterest you from doing God's good will.

Take adult pornography for example. Magazine pages, cable TV and web sites are filled with all sorts of attractive women, beautiful bodies, suggestive poses and erotic stories. Years ago, one had to seek out porn in a convenience store or seedy video store on the other side of town. Today, pornography is more mainstream and comes into our homes and offices through our computers, cable TVs and DVD players. People no longer have to go out looking for porn—it finds them. Want to know how prevalent porn is? Type in the word "sex" on an Internet search engine and you'll get millions of adult-based web sites in under a half second. Or check the quantity of adult only pay-per-views you can purchase on your home TV or in your family's hotel room. Now just a click of your mouse or aim of your remote cues up instant and insatiable temptation. If you don't stand against Satan's schemes, the desire to check it out grows even more tantalizing because porn is always "on" and so readily accessible.

At first glance, Satan tricks some into thinking pornography is innocent enough, and many fine, upstanding men and women believe there's nothing really wrong with it as long as consenting adults and no minors are involved. But look beyond its deceitful allure, however, and you'll see pornography exploits and demeans women, destroys relationships and families, promotes pedophilia and corrupts the minds and imaginations of impressionable teens. In fact, porn is so invasive and habitual that it is sometimes referred to as the "crack cocaine" epidemic of the new millennium.

Never underestimate the power Satan has to corrupt your mind, body and soul. Satan dresses up temptation to look all nice and pretty like a big, irresistible gift package, but the surprise is often on you. When you peel away its alluring facade, what's inside doesn't always look quite as attractive and isn't nearly as satisfying as you expected it to be. Just like corporate advertisements and promotions, Satan's offers frequently involve greed, lust, sex, vanity and ego to snare your attention and entrap you. Chances are, you've fallen for a few of his gratuitous follies and are worse off for it.

## Satan Corrupts All Christians

Just think of all the ways Satan targets you for sin and temptation. Consider the Christian who would never venture into an adult video store in a million years, but casually looks at Internet pornography at home or work when no one else is around. Or what about the otherwise honest Christian who mistakenly receives an extra $20 in change and justifies keeping that ill-gotten gain by rationalizing they need the money more than the store does? Or the Christian who has lustful thoughts about another's spouse, a married coworker or some stranger on the commuter train? Or the Christian business owner who justifies unethical practices or cutting corners as vital to success in the marketplace?

That Satan, he's a fiendishly clever devil alright. Not only does he package temptation up nice and neat, he also makes strategic and surgical strikes at your weakest point, frequently taking aim at your fears, frustrations and insecurities. In Ephesians 6:13, Paul exhorts believers to put on the full armor of God "so that when the day of evil comes, you may be able to stand your ground."

But, standing your ground is sometimes difficult to do. All of us are inherently weak and even the strongest Christians have chinks in their armor that Satan will gladly exploit. He knows where your fallacies lie and slowly but surely whittles away at them until you either shore up your defenses or surrender to the temptations assaulting you. Take a good look at yourself and be honest. You know your weak spot and where the chink in your armor lies. So don't just stand there and let Satan beat you down. Reach out for Christ, bring out your spiritual repair kit and bolster those chinks so you can get back to advertising God to your maximum potential.

When writing this book, I felt Satan doing everything he could to prevent me from doing the work God called me to do. When I'd run up against a creative brick wall and struggle with the right way to communicate an idea, Satan was surely delighted thinking I might grow frustrated enough to stop writing altogether and just chuck the book in the trash. When that didn't work, he tried to divert my focus from the glorious opportunity and privilege God had entrusted me with towards thinking about the enormous challenge of writing, editing, publishing and marketing a book. Other times it was computer games or sheer laziness that diverted my attention from writing. In other words, Satan did whatever it took to keep me from doing something good for God. Regrettably, his tactics worked and he was sometimes successful distracting me and getting me off Christ's task. But, for the most part, Satan's ploys backfired because I decided early on that if he was working that hard to discourage me from writing, I must have been doing something really pleasing to God. Which made me all the more determined to press on despite Satan's diversions.

When it comes to advertising God, I'm convinced that God doesn't call any of us to undertake a project in order to see us fail. Yes, the task before us sometimes seems so monumentally difficult, but if you stay true to God's calling, I believe He will provide you with the way and the means to get it done. Don't allow Satan's lies and trickery to convince you otherwise or distract you from a God-directed task. When you feel Satan's deceit threatening to lure you away from God, take the promise of James 4:7 to heart—"Submit yourselves, then, to God. Resist the devil and he will flee from you." Oh sure, just like the Terminator, Satan will be back alright, but each time you repel him, the stronger and more confident you'll become warding off temptations so you can stand firm in the ways of the Lord.

## 10. You Think Advertising God Isn't Politically Correct

Exactly when the era of political correctness, or PC, actually began seems open to debate. Some assert it's been going on for years as language evolves to coincide with the prevailing social climate of the times. Others say it began more recently as the result of an orchestrated government agenda or overly sensitive minorities and special interest groups. While some aspects of political correctness may be socially beneficial when it comes to tolerance, cultural sensitivities or improving race relations, PC becomes just plain silly when Christians use it as an excuse for not sharing their faith or failing to advertise God out of a fear they might offend someone or experience themselves some form of social reprisal.

Jesus Christ certainly didn't conform to the PC teachings of His day, nor did the possibility of offending prominent and influential religious teachers, leaders and priests prevent Jesus from preaching the truthful word of God. Moreover, Jesus didn't mince His words or soften God's message to make it more palatable for those hearing it. And Jesus certainly didn't shy away from showing compassion to people society deemed undesirable and unworthy. Jesus didn't seek to conform to society's rules and regulations, He sought only to do the will of the Father, whatever it was and wherever it took Him.

Unfortunately, some churches and Christians today can't say the same thing about themselves. We scoff at political correctness, yet allow it to constrain and inhibit our words and actions for Christ. We allow our core Christian beliefs and values to be compromised by the ever-encroaching stigma of being politically correct. We allow society, media outlets and government officials to dictate what we can say and when and where we can say it, and let them chastise us when our words and actions go against the prevailing PC sentiment. For example, many public school systems and universities can no longer have community or team prayer before a football game nor deliver an invocation at graduation because these actions conflict with the separation of church and state. Many prominent retailers discourage their employees from saying "Merry Christmas" for fear such a blatantly religiously-laden message could somehow alienate or horribly offend those who don't celebrate Christmas. When a public figure or celebrity speaks out against hot button topics like abortion or homosexuality, the media and special interest groups often vilify them and accuse the person of maliciousness, bigotry and hatemongering.

The agents of Satan have become far too successful at silencing our Christian voices. Again, I ask you to go back and read Galatians 1:10. When it comes to spreading the word of God, you're here to please Christ, not groups, employers, media outlets, courts, your family or anyone else. You're here to promote the love and salvation of Jesus Christ regardless of whether others deem it to be politically correct or not.

My wife and I recently heard an interview with a famous adult movie megastar where she was asked if she thought she was going to heaven. Without hesitation and with complete confidence, she replied absolutely she would go to heaven.

Her justification? She believed that in spite of her occupation she was a good person at heart. When asked the same question, her husband, her agent and several friends agreed the porn star had a kind heart and a good soul and would be in heaven. To me, they seemed to take the attitude that God would be fortunate to have her there. I was totally shocked. Whatever happened to professing belief in Jesus Christ, repenting of your sins and accepting Him unequivocally as the savior of your life? Granted, the actress could have professed her relationship with Christ in a segment that was edited out, but I seriously doubt it or she wouldn't continue to be a prime purveyor of porn and soldier of Satan.

But, the porn star isn't the only person out there who honestly believes a good heart and good deeds will secure them a place in heaven. That kind of feel good mentality is running amuck in our society. There are plenty of really good and loving people out there who do the kind-hearted work of Christ and may even express a belief in God. The problem is, they never truly and humbly accept Christ into their lives and therefore, according to John 14:6, cannot come to the Father. In James 2:19, the disciple acknowledges that even demons believe in God, but they don't obey Him.

I didn't really expect the interviewer to challenge the validity and rationale of the porn actress's false beliefs, but when we hear misstatements similar to hers spoken in our circle of friends, coworkers and acquaintances, we need to stand up for God by lovingly and Scripturally correcting them. You don't do them any favors by softening God's message or letting incorrect beliefs they have go unchallenged out of some misplaced allegiance to political correctness instead of obedience to God.

All too frequently in today's world, Christians are not the influencers of public perception; rather, they themselves are too heavily influenced by the world's standards and its peoples, popularity and culture. Nothing's changed. It's been that way for thousands of years. Compromising your faith or weakening your message for the sake of pleasing other people may be deemed sensitive and politically correct by humans, but it is not Godly correct. And it is God's view of what we say and do that ultimately counts.

As Christians called to advertise God, we simply cannot allow the blanket of political correctness to smother and extinguish the light of Christ that shines within us. God doesn't put limitations on when and where we should advertise Him and, as I just mentioned, He certainly doesn't want us to water down His message so as not to offend someone. In the Bible, prophets and lowly servants confronted mighty kings, John called out Herod for sleeping with Herod's brother's wife and Jesus challenged the religious leaders over their hypocrisy. The fact is, we should be "offending" people by confronting them with their nonchalant attitudes about sin and disobedience to God instead of pandering to them with kid gloves so as not to hurt their feelings.

But, because all of us sin and sin frequently, it's hard to cast those stones at others without coming across as having a "holier than thou" attitude or as judgmental. And the truth is, you do have to be careful. Jesus cautions us about this in Luke 6:41-42 when He says, "Why do you look at the speck of sawdust in your brother's eye and pay no attention in your own eye? First, take the plank out of your eye, and then you will see clearly to remove the speck from your brother's eye." Don't follow this Scripture and not only do you lose credibility, some will deem you a hypocrite and point their finger right back at you.

You know you can never live a life completely free of sin, but that doesn't mean you shouldn't help others recognize, remedy and accept responsibility for theirs, even as you try to remove the speck of sin from your own life. No one likes to be called on the carpet for their actions, but it is part of our Christian culture and Biblical teachings to love, nurture, instruct and even rebuke one another when necessary. It's hard to live a Christ-centered, Christ-focused life by ourselves. That's why, like raising our children, we need help fighting temptation so we can focus our full attention on Christ. We need strengthening from other Christians who hold us accountable for our words and actions and get on us for our lack of saying and doing things for God.

Society and peers alike exert an enormous amount of pressure on everyone, Christians and non-believers alike, to conform. But God doesn't want Christians to cower to societal pressures or reside in dark, shadowy corners to avoid the possibility of rejection or humiliation. On the contrary, God wants you to stand up for Jesus and stand out from the crowd. He wants you to come out into the light for all to see and boldly proclaim and advertise the lifesaving Christian message whenever we can. Sometimes, it's easy. Many times it is not. The next time you find yourself reluctant to speak up for God, recall Paul's words in Ephesians 5:1 and 5:15-20 and cheerfully praise God in any and all situations, whether it's politically correct or not.

## UP FOR DISCUSSION.

1.   What fears do you have when it comes to advertising God?

2.   If all Christians are sinners, are all Christians hypocrites?

3.  Why is it easier to go with the flow than go against the tide, especially when it comes to advertising God?

4.  Why is reading the Bible so easy to put on the back burner?

5.  Do you find you live a 9 to 5, Monday to Friday existence? Where does serving God fit into your lifestyle?

6.  What "chinks" do you have in your armor? What can you do to fend off Satan's attacks and take your stand against his schemes?

7.  Do you feel political correctness limits or impedes your ability and desire to advertise God? How?

# 9

## *Sin and Advertising God*

o o o o o o o o o o o o o o o o o o o o o o o o o o o o o o o o o o o

"Do not use your freedom to indulge the sinful nature, rather, serve one another."

—{ *Galatians 5:13* }

Like a virus or infectious disease, sin poisons our bodies, pollutes our minds and impedes our relationship with Jesus Christ. Sometimes sin is blatant and painfully obvious. Other times, it's so subtle that you go on about your business and maybe never even realize you've sinned. Want to know God's position on sin? Paul gives you the answer in no uncertain terms in Romans 8:8 when he writes, "Those controlled by the sinful nature cannot please God." But, Paul immediately follows up in verse 9 with the more encouraging words, "You, however, are controlled not by the sinful nature but by the Spirit, if the Spirit of God lives in you." Paul expounds on this statement in Galatians 5:16-18 when he writes, "So I say, live by the Spirit, and you will not gratify the desires of the sinful nature. For the sinful nature desires what is contrary to the Spirit, and the Spirit what is contrary to the sinful nature. They are in conflict with one another, so that you do not do what you want." If the Spirit of God lives in you, and I pray that it does, then you will have a stronger desire to let God lead you instead of clinging to and following your sinful tendencies.

That's easy to say, but harder sometimes to do. That's because sin is sort of like running a red light. You know you're supposed to stop at the light, and maybe even intend to stop, but you have this stubborn streak that causes you to ignore that bright red signal and accelerate forward because it's what you want to do, not what the authority of the traffic light is telling you to do. Isn't that the way it is with sin? You know you should stop doing something, but you continue on saying this or doing that without slamming on the brakes even when the sign is there imploring you to come to a screeching halt.

In reality, sin is so prevalent in our lives that it's not uncommon to go from a moment of closeness with God and fall immediately into a sinful action the next. We've all been there and done that. Think about the profanity you yelled out in frustration while playing a tennis match just a few hours after church. Consider the racy cable TV program you watched after saying your nightly prayer. Or when you look up from reading your Bible on your lunch break and an unloving thought crosses your mind about a coworker who just passed your office door. These little things may not seem like much, but the apostle John declares, "All wrongdoing is sin" in 1 John 5:17.

No one said it was easy being a follower of Christ. It's a real challenge to faithfully adhere to Christ's teachings day in and day out. Your mind occasionally strays into ungodly territory. Your words sometimes belie your relationship with Christ. Your actions are often times in direct conflict with your true beliefs. And Satan's constant schemes and deceits only add to the difficulty of standing firm in your faith.

## I Sin, You Sin, We All Sin

Some say that in order to gauge a person's true character all you have to do is watch them when they are completely alone to see what choices they make. And for some, this could be rather embarrassing at times. Jesus said those who live in the dark don't want the light shining on them for fear their deeds and actions will be exposed for all to see. It makes sense. Consider your own life when you're at home and no one else is around, or when you're alone in your hotel room on a business trip. Who do you socialize with? What do you watch on TV? What websites do you visit? What books and magazines do you read? If your spouse, child, friend or someone from your church unexpectedly dropped in, what would they think about the things you were doing or the company you were keeping? Would it be in conflict with your Christian beliefs? As someone striving to advertise God, would you be practicing all the things you preach? Or would you be the one happily tearing into all those cleverly wrapped boxes of "sin" we talked about earlier?

Sometimes I think it's a little of both. It seems plenty of us have one face we'll put on for friends and family and another, more guarded one we show to those we don't know very well. When it comes to being a Christian witness, however, you should only have one consistent face on display. So what kind of image do you portray as a Christian serving God? Do you come across as all pious and perfect or as a humble sinner in constant need of God's forgiveness and grace? If you're truly abiding by God's teachings, your answer should be the latter. Because you're attuned to and guided by Scripture, you are well aware that sin lurks inside the hearts and minds of all people, and no matter how hard you try to abide by the teachings of Jesus Christ, you not going to escape the reach of sin or alter the reality of its daily existence.

I'm not saying you don't have control over temptation and deciding whether or not to participate in a sinful action because you absolutely do. God gives us the free will to make the choice between right and wrong. It's just that, in this world, sin is an ugly inevitably since we are always going to be weaker in the flesh than we are stronger in the Spirit. Only when we go to live with God in heaven will sin truly be forever purged and vanquished. Thank God for the compassionate grace of Jesus Christ who lovingly frees us from the shackles of sin!

The truth is, even on your very best days, even when you feel genuine closeness with the Lord, you continue to commit sin because of a flawed obedience to God. You can wake up one morning and say you're not going to sin all day, but you have no chance to succeed because Satan ensured ours would be a sinful world when he corrupted Adam and Eve back in the garden. And while thankfully, we have immunity from sin's deadly consequences by the compassionate love and immense grace of our Lord Jesus Christ, none of us get through life unblemished by the stain of sin. Not you, not your children, not your neighbor, not your minister, not even the Pope himself. We are all born imperfect. We do not learn or develop imperfection. If you think otherwise, you are only fooling yourself. In Psalm 51:5, David recognized the depth of sin within by acknowledging, "Surely I was sinful at birth, sinful from the time my mother conceived me."

We all want to protect ourselves from sinning as best we can, but try as we might, we simply cannot escape temptation or our predisposition to committing sin. It's like the homeowner who wants to protect her house. She deadbolts all the doors and locks all the windows, but can't secure a back door. It remains unlocked, inviting evildoers to enter and plunder inside. It's the same way with us. We can go to church every Sunday, diligently read the Bible, pray daily and immerse ourselves in Godly works, but sin will still find a "back door inside" because we cannot lock up our minds, words and thoughts in an absolutely failsafe way. Sin has this clever way of finding unsecured points of entry and creeping in when our guard is down.

But just because you fall short of perfection and God's glory doesn't mean God wants you to use your deficiencies as an excuse or a crutch to fall back on so you can get out of doing the things God requires of you. Mahatma Gandhi once said "my imperfections and failures are as much a blessing from God as my successes and my talents and I lay them both at his feet."[16] Although you can't live a perfect life free from the tarnish of sin, you can and should strive to be more loving and Christ-like every day. Never use your inclination to sin as an excuse for not advertising God, failing to follow His commands or to avoid doing the work God calls you to do.

## Sin is a Natural By-Product of Our Disobedience to God

In my younger days, I was one of those diehard TV wrestling junkies. I couldn't get enough of the back breakers, big leg kicks, rude awakenings and outrageous subplots staged in and out of the ring. To me, the matches were a metaphor for life, complete with good vs. evil, painful falls and knockdowns, and triumph over adversity. And then there were the villains, the mean and nasty bad-guy wrestlers that all the fans and even the announcers loved to hate.

For me, sin is a lot like those mean-spirited wrestling villains. It's ugly, intimidating and downright despicable. Sin flagrantly breaks the rules by taunting you, kicking you when you're down, and even smacks down others who come to your rescue. Sin can often seem invincible, too big and too powerful to overcome. You may put up a good fight for awhile, but sin has a knack for finding and exploiting your weak spot, eventually knocking you off your feet and pinning you down. Occasionally, you may be strong enough to fend off sin for a few rounds, but like the cagey and unrelenting villain who knows no quit, sin is a fierce competitor and won't give up easily either. It's like a never-ending match and you can pretty well figure on sin coming back to wrestle with your conscience and test your spiritual strength again and again.

If the wrestling example doesn't grab you, maybe this parallel from history will. In medieval Europe, cities would come under frequent attack from foreign invaders looking to conquer the land. City walls were fortified, entry points were secured and barricaded, and sentinels were posted to keep watch day and night for potential trouble. Just like marauders in feudal times, sin too constantly seeks to invade the walls of your mind and body. Maintaining a watchful eye will help you see sin approaching, but strengthening your defenses through steadfast prayer, meditation and the reading of God's Word is what will help you keep certain sins from breaking through your fortifications. I use the phrase "certain sins" because, no matter how tough or resilient your stronghold is, your natural imperfections will never allow you to utterly beat back sin in this life. Only the triumphant and glorious return of Jesus Christ and His subsequent victory over Satan will signal the end of all evil and sin forever. And when that time comes, it's like the old gospel hymn says, what a day of rejoicing that will be!

## Is It Just Me?

Sometimes, it's easy to feel like you're the only one who wrestles with sin every day of your life. That you're the only one who feels like you're not the model Christian you strive so hard to be. You may even wonder if other people encounter the same trials and temptations as you, but find yourself too embarrassed to seek them out and ask how they deal with these issues. It's easy for me to say you shouldn't be self-conscious, but really, you shouldn't be. Jesus tells us that anyone who is without sin should cast the first stones. Paul reminds us in Romans 3:23 that "we all have sinned and fallen short of God's glory." And when Paul says "we" he's talking about everyone, including all the great heroes of the Bible such as Moses, Abraham, David, Elijah, Peter, John, even himself.

All these individuals were great men of the faith, yet they were human beings just like you and I with definite weaknesses and fallacies, some of which the Bible points out. And though Paul, perhaps history's greatest apostle, refers to himself as the worst of all sinners in 1 Timothy 1:15 and "less than the least of all of God's people" in Ephesians 3:8, just look at all the wondrous ways in which God used him to hasten the spread of the early church and how his New Testament letters were and remain a vital source of spiritual teaching, inspiration and instruction for millions of Christians.

The point is all of us have sins that get the better of us. It was that way in Biblical times and it's that way now. And sometimes, the only way to get the help we need to combat those sins is to make ourselves more vulnerable and admit our weaknesses to a friend, counselor or pastor we trust, who in turn can direct us to the help we need. Sure it's tough to confess sins, especially those that are embarrassing or that have the potential to hurt or affect others. But don't burden yourself with the weight of unforgiven sin. Nothing you do separates you from the bigness of God's love, redemption and forgiving grace.

But because sin continues to rage on even after forgiveness and repentance, many Christians mistakenly feel they are not worthy of God's grace or qualified to advertise His love. It's not that they don't love the Lord, don't want to serve Him or don't have a deep passion for seeing others come to Christ. Rather, their feelings of inadequacy prevent them from sharing their faith with the authority and confidence God calls for. I know plenty of determined Christians who want to be good ambassadors of the faith and representatives of their church, but because sin runs rampant in their lives, they feel they simply cannot in good conscience be a voice for Christ or consistently project the image that true repentance and salvation call for. Because they struggle with feelings of hypocrisy, they don't consider themselves the best ones to offer spiritual advice or work to influence others in a positive way. They reason that if they can't keep their own sin in check, then who are they to share their faith with others.

If that sums up the way you feel, don't be so hard on yourself. We all come to God from different vantage points and life experiences. No one is worthy to receive God's immeasurable love, grace and forgiveness on their own, yet God still doles it out freely and in never ceasing abundance. That kind of agape love is hard to fathom really, especially when you realize that God's free love isn't just reserved exclusively for His faithful followers. God loves everyone the same, including the ones society deems unlovable like hardened inmates, AIDS patients, prostitutes, drug addicts, the homeless, even murderous terrorists. We may not like it and we may not understand it, but God loves them all, and all of them are available for inclusion into His heavenly kingdom once they accept Christ and repent of their sins.

## Talk About Temptation

I don't believe it is a sin to be tempted. Temptation only turns to sin when we act on it. After all, Satan tempted Jesus Christ on at least three separate occasions that we know of, yet Jesus remained free from sin. We all have our weak spots that make certain temptations super hard to resist. Sometimes temptation dangles before us like a rich, moist piece of homemade chocolate cake, its decadence beckoning us to give in and indulge. Much like recovering addicts are taught to avoid situations where alcohol or drugs will be present, Christians must learn to identify problem areas and distance themselves from the people, places or thoughts that trigger temptation. In 1 Corinthians 10:13, Paul declares, "God is faithful; He will not let you be tempted beyond what you can bear. But when you are tempted, He will also provide a way out so that you can stand up under it." It's extremely reassuring to know you can always go to God for help during troubling times.

Instead of giving in to sin, try this prayer the next time you need stability and encouragement in the face of temptation.

*Merciful Almighty God, give me the strength I need to fight the evil before me. Cup my chin in your loving hands, and lift my eyes towards the things of heaven instead of the things of earth. And prevent my gaze from dropping low, O God, so that I don't stare down into the pit of sin. Train my eyes up to your grace and to your call, dear*

*God, so that I am made stronger in the Spirit instead of weaker in the flesh. Help me to grow into a more loving and abundant relationship with you. Amen.*

## Recognize and Confess Your Sinful Nature

Becoming more Christ-like requires a change of heart and sincere repentance. It means, among other things, claiming and utilizing your spiritual gifts, developing a servant's humble attitude, putting the needs of others first, and following the path God wants you to take in life and in servitude. Sometimes, it can be difficult to know whether the road and actions you choose are determined by God's divine will or by your own selfish motivations. God is supremely benevolent and gives all of us the freedom of choice to make our own decisions. Sometimes our actions are in harmony with God's will; other times, they are not. Either way, make no mistake—it is these crucial decisions of what we say, what we do and where we choose to go that ultimately make or break our relationship with God.

I'm always amazed at how many Christians, or those with whom you're advertising God, have such a hard time recognizing and identifying their sin and weaknesses. People who can't see the truth or won't accept the fact they are sinners are like those who refuse to acknowledge or seek treatment for a serious addiction or illness. They're never going to get any better by living in denial about the lifestyle or activities that's harmful to their physical and spiritual well being. Recognizing and confessing that you are a sinner is one of the first steps in relinquishing your life to Christ so He and He alone can free you from the chains of sin past, present and future.

But whether it's due to pride and stubbornness or both, admitting sin is something that's difficult for many people, believers and unbelievers alike, to do at times. Maybe it's because they have to admit their mistakes and they don't like to be wrong. We see early on how society values the strength of its heroes and mocks the foibles and vices of the weak. That's why we cheer the triumphs of athletes and entertainers, but scoff at the troubles of the downtrodden.

Conceding your weaknesses and shortcomings can make you feel vulnerable, guilty and ashamed. Such confessions can make you feel like you're not as strong, not as good and not as pious a person as you would like and would like others to believe. Instead of allowing vanity and pride to prevent you from owning up to your sins, recognize that guilt, shame and vincibility are key in establishing genuine humility and sincere repentance. God wants us to come to Him with a heavy heart similar to David in Psalm 51:1-2 where he cries out, "Have mercy on me, O God, according to your unfailing love...blot out my transgressions. Wash away all my iniquity and cleanse me from my sin."

Still, even though you sin and are forgiven by God, you're a sinner, no better or worse than any other sinner in the world. You can't make yourself look better in the eyes of God by comparing the depth and degree of your sins to those of others. You can't justify your sinful actions by saying things like "sure, I may take a few deductions I'm not entitled to on my income tax return, but at least I don't rob banks," or "maybe I have a dirty little thought about my neighbor's wife every now and then, but at least I'm not sleeping with her," or "okay, so I look the other way when a homeless person needs help, at least I'm not the one who forced him out into the street."

With the exception of the unforgivable sin Jesus mentions in Luke 12:10, I don't think God ranks the severity of sin from minor misstep to major infraction. In God's eyes, sin isn't graded on the human scale of bad to worse. God doesn't see things the same way we do nor does He have those "gray" areas. To Him, a sin is a sin is a sin. To call it anything less than that or make excuses or blame others for our actions isn't consistent with having a contrite heart.

We all know real repentance isn't easy. And, more often than not, repentance is not achieved in one giant leap, but in smaller baby steps. I like to think God understands that. Omnipotent and omnipresent, He knows what is in our heart and mind and whether or not we're really trying to avoid temptation and sin. He understands we will stumble, but I think God wants us to call on Him so we can get back on track and refocused on Him instead of latching on to our failures and weaknesses.

## Develop a Disdain for Sin

We know that only through the intercession of Jesus Christ are we able to have true reconciliation with God and claim the promise of eternal life. In 1 John 3:8-9, the apostle proclaims, "He who does what is sinful is of the devil because the devil has been sinning from the beginning…No one who is born of God will continue to sin because God's seed remains in him; he cannot go on sinning because he has been born of God." As a child of God, you are always looking to gain victory over sin instead of justifying your sinful action again and again with no honest inclination to change. I interpret John's preceding verse to mean that you don't stop sinning just because you accept Christ. If anything, temptation probably gets worse for you because Satan realizes you're drawing closer to God and away from him so he wants you back. Like we talked about, Satan wants to reclaim you as one of his "customers" and will do everything in his power to see that it happens. So expect temptation to increase and prepare for it by strengthening your resolve through prayer and by studying and immersing yourself in God's Holy Word.

But repentant Christians who desire to live in harmony with the teachings of Christ will take sincere steps to discontinue their sinful ways. They don't wallow in self-pity and make excuses for not advertising God. In other words, to be righteous, you must seek to live righteously. The difference between true Christians and those who haven't fully dedicated their life to Christ is true Christians genuinely work towards defeating their sinful ways because they have God's "seed" of new life in them through their faith in Jesus Christ. By seeking God's will first and making a life-altering decision to conscientiously avoid people, places and situations that offer irresistible temptations, Christians can develop a genuine disdain for sin and turn their life in a new direction, one that brings them closer to God and farther away from the sins and temptations that once ensnared them.

Romans 12:9 instructs us to, "Hate what is evil; cling to what is good." If you're serious about getting the upper hand on temptation and sin, you must develop a true hatred for sin. I'm talking about the kind of hatred that makes you angry with yourself and your vulnerabilities. The kind of hatred that makes you flat out determined to make a change in how you live and how you approach and obey God. It's like breaking a bad habit. You eventually get so fed up with the dependency on that habit that one day you get mad enough to stop it and promise yourself you're never going to do it again.

There's probably a particular sin or two you continue to struggle with. Maybe it's the same few things that tempt you every day or perhaps something you wrestle with only occasionally. Yet tempt you it does. And if you're like me, there are times you pray for strength and receive the courage from the Holy Spirit to successfully fight off the temptation. But, there's also those days where the urge to engage in that sin is infinitely stronger and far more appealing than the willpower you have to resist it. In other words, there's nothing that's going to stand in your way and prevent you from giving in to that sinful desire. You rationalize the sin in your mind to appease your conscience, then go ahead and do whatever it is you know God doesn't want you to do. You may even think about praying for help, but in the end decide not to. Only after you commit the sin do you feel really ashamed and guilt-ridden knowing you should have cried out to the Lord for strength and encouragement. Don't feel like it's just you. Christians on every faith level have been there and done that. And usually hate how badly they feel afterwards. So get angry with yourself. Hate what you've done. Hate that you allowed Satan to lull you into that sinful place. Hate that you didn't lean on God more. Then, channel that hatred in a positive way so when you're strongly tempted again, that disdain helps you steer clear from trouble.

## Sin Happens

Because of our propensity to sin, we let God down every single day. We lapse into sinful thoughts, words and actions even when we don't mean to, even when we're trying really hard not to. Do you ever feel like you're stuck in a continual cycle of sin and ask forgiveness, sin and ask forgiveness? I know I do, and I feel sure it's fairly common to most Christians. The prayer of forgiveness you ask is probably one you can recite by heart since you've said it so many times before.

I don't have to tell you giving in to sin is easy. It's the standing firm and resisting part that is so difficult at times. Some sins, such as profanity, apathy, laziness and gossiping are merely bad habits and attributes you can correct. Some sins, like shunning those who are different or showing callousness to those in need, are conditioned responses that require a wholesale attitude adjustment. Sins such as these can be controlled, even eliminated with a repentant heart. Remember Jesus' second greatest commandment from Matthew 22:39? It instructs you to love one another as yourself. Take a look at 1 John 3:10 to see how the disciple's words echo Christ's commandment and how ardently John feels about sin and indifference to your fellow humans. The verse reads, "This is how we know who the children of God are and who the children of the devil are: anyone who does not do what is right is not a child of God; nor is anyone who does not love his brother." Strong words to consider when adjusting our sinful attitudes.

Fortunately, we worship a God who understands what it is like to be fully human because He came to earth as a real man with real personality and emotions. Referring to Christ, the writer of Hebrews says in 2:18, "Because He himself suffered when He was tempted, He is able to help those who are being tempted." Later in Hebrews 4:15, the writer emphasizes that "we do not have a high priest who is unable to sympathize with our weaknesses, but we have one who has been tempted in every way just as we are." Jesus knows what we go through because He went through temptation himself.

God knows we are not perfect, but He loves us in spite of that. He wants us to grow into productive disciples by offering endless forgiveness along with practical Biblical wisdom that can help us overcome the tempting lure of sin. Rather than continually beating yourself up over sinful actions, pray for forgiveness and work hard to repent. Avoid places and situations that encourage sin. Take lessons learned from your mistakes and use them as a positive influence for others.

Sometimes you don't set out to advertise God, but then one day, you find yourself in the company of someone who struggles with the same sins and weaknesses you do. Perhaps God has put you in this very position for this very reason—to share the story of how God's forgiveness helped you overcome similar obstacles. God's purpose for you could very well lie in how a triumph over your own weakness ultimately gave you the courage, empathy and strength to reach out and help others in the same boat. Being a sinner gives you unique insight into God's ever-abundant grace and allows you to help others rise above their own imperfections and find redemption in Christ. You just never know what God has in store for you until you grab hold of your faith and run with it.

Because you yourself have experienced Christ's forgiveness from sin firsthand, you are in a great position to advertise God with powerful and personal conviction. Don't keep that kind of good news to yourself—passionately testify to Christ's truth and forgiveness whenever you have the opportunity. You're always going to grapple with sin and temptation. You can't do anything about that. But what you can do is not let your penchant to sin become a humongous weight you drag around day after day and let it hold you back from testifying and professing your love for Christ. Let God use your sinful experiences and the lessons you've learned from those experiences to impact and encourage positive change in others.

## UP FOR DISCUSSION.

1.  In which areas of your life do you struggle with sin? What can you do differently? What do you do when you feel really tempted?

2.  How does your own struggle against sin help you better advertise God?

3.  Do people respect Christians who readily admit to their sins? Does it make Christians more credible witnesses? Or does it give unbelievers more reasons to not be like us?

4.  Do you think most people "recognize" their sins? Why or why not? What are some ways you can move people from denial to repentance?

5.  How can you train yourself to "hate" sin?

# 10

## *Negatively Advertising God*

○ ○ ○ ○ ○ ○ ○ ○ ○ ○ ○ ○ ○ ○ ○ ○ ○ ○ ○ ○ ○ ○ ○ ○ ○ ○ ○ ○ ○

"And you will again see the distinction between the righteous and the wicked, between those who serve God and those that do not."

—{ *Malachi 3:18* }

Although market research shows the majority of consumers don't care much for negative advertising, it nonetheless continues to be part of America's mainstream corporate philosophy. Think about it. How many ads do you see or hear where company A says something less than flattering about rival company B? Consider the ads where one car company touts the safety record of its vehicle over the less flattering ones of its competitor's. Or an antacid product advertising it has doctor-recommended calcium while its rival's does not. In both instances, companies highlight the negative to accentuate the positive. Negative advertising is also quite common during political election seasons where one candidate intentionally maligns the character or distorts the voting record of his or her opponent.

But, let's not be so quick to jump on corporate America and our esteemed politicians for sometimes painting a less than stellar picture of another. Look in the mirror and be honest with yourself. Have you ever pointed out flaws in a coworker's performance to help advance your career? Do you ever justify your own questionable actions by comparing them to those of others who do far worse deeds? Do you ever distort facts, gossip or use someone's words out of context to make yourself look better? Have you ever pointed the finger at someone else instead of accepting responsibility for a mistake you made? From a Christian perspective, that's negative advertising too.

The majority of this book focuses on all the positive ways we can and should be out there advertising God. Unfortunately, human nature being what is, sinful, stubborn and rebellious, we find ourselves guilty of advertising God in plenty of negative ways, too. Obedient, well-intending Christians obviously don't purposely set out on a campaign of negative advertising. It's just that, like we saw in the previous chapter, we all have this thing called sin that invades our bodies, poisons our minds and causes our words and actions to occasionally go horribly awry and out of sync with God's wishes. Sometimes, our negative advertisements about God are so unintentional and so seemingly innocuous that they may slip right by without our notice. But, just because we fail to recognize the detrimental things we say and do doesn't mean others don't take note of our gaffes and slip-ups.

In blogging communities on the Internet, there's a whole sub-culture of people out there who love to catch and publicize every little mistake in the continuity of a film or TV show. It's amazing just how alert and astute these viewers are. They notice even the simplest miscues such as one character calling another by a different name, how a hat is on, then off, then back on again from one scene to the next, and incorrect geographic references. How they catch most of these errors I'll never know, but as you browse the web sites of your favorite show or movie, you see these diehard videophiles don't miss much because they are always on the lookout for a mistake.

So it is, I think, with those watching your every Christian move. These casual and not-so-casual observers take notice of your mistakes, even the simple ones, and may even go so far as to point those miscues out to your face or to others in the form of gossiping. Maybe it's a fellow Christian who sees what you do or hears what you say and silently disapproves from afar. Or, maybe it's someone new in their faith that has a hard time understanding how your words and actions coincide with the teachings of Christ, or how your support for a certain cause or group is in harmony with moral and ethical positions of the Christian church. Or maybe it's someone who is totally apathetic to Christ and you've just added more fuel to their fire because they view you as a hypocrite for professing to be a Christian, but not living like one. None of these preceding examples is a good road for Christians to wander down. As advertisers of God, we want to promote the positives of living a life for God and unapologetically serving the Lord, not create the opposite effect by saying or doing something negative that contradicts everything we stand for and believe in.

## Negative Advertising Belies our True Purpose and Fosters False Notions about Christianity

There's a very common misconception among many non-believers that Christians suddenly become perfect angels once they are saved. It's not true of course, but some Christians inadvertently advance the stereotype by acting like they're better than everyone else. Or as we saw in Chapter 9, they mistakenly convince themselves that their sins are somehow not as bad as another's, especially when they try to justify that sin by framing it within a certain context or shielding the impact of their sin under the umbrella they call "the grand scheme of things." If you fall into these categories, you might be negatively advertising God.

Take a look at what Jesus says about judging in Matthew 7:1-5. No Christian is qualified to act haughty or cast judgment on or disparage others because we always have some kind of sawdust or plank in our own eyes that needs to be tended to. Leave the plank there and it blinds us to the compassionate love we are taught to share with others. Such inaction and hypocrisy on our part in turn only reinforces the negative opinion many of skeptical and apathetic non-believers may already have of us. So why give them any more ammunition?

It bears repeating—no one is immune from sin. Come across as a person who looks down your nose at the sins of others while not addressing the "plank" that is your own sinful action, and not only are you not following the teachings of Christ, you're also negatively advertising God by conveying to others that you've elevated yourself to a spiritual position you most definitely do not warrant. At the end of the day, you're a sinner just like everyone else, no better, no worse.

Early in my adult faith, I participated in a Bible study class with a dozen or so other believers. My beliefs were still a little shaky and unclear, so I was a bit intimidated by what I perceived to be a more faith-mature Christian group. Because they all appeared to be fine, upstanding Christians and devoted church members, I honestly thought their lives were somehow exempt from stress, problems and personal conflicts. Deep down, I felt like they were all just plain better than me because they appeared to be so deep-rooted and committed to their faith beliefs.

Spiritually, I knew I wasn't on the same par with them, and I felt apprehensive about sharing my opinions on the Scriptures we had to read. However, after a few weeks of often candid discussion about specific Bible passages and how those verses applied to our own understandings and lifestyles, I gradually began to see that these people were not so different from me after all. They did things they weren't supposed to do. They blew off volunteering in the church. They muttered four-letter words at other drivers in traffic. In other words, they sinned, they stressed, they exhibited poor Christian character at times. Imagine that. My naivety is humorous now, but what an eye-opening revelation it was for me back then!

Rather than the perfect little Christians I mistakenly labeled them, I discovered they were real people struggling with real problems and searching for real answers by studying and discussing Christ's word. Just like me. Although they were loyal churchgoers who read, studied and applied God's word to their lives, they still possessed many of the same questions, doubts, temptations and struggles I did. It was a watershed moment in my faith life because I came to see that none of us in that group was really very different at all. In fact, I found I had more in common with them than I originally thought. We all fell short of God's glory every day, but we also shared a genuine love for Jesus Christ and an earnest desire to live better for Him. We just professed and applied that love in different ways based on our life experiences and personalities. Sometime during the course of that nine-month-long Bible study, it struck me that God didn't make perfect humans. Rather, God perfected his love and grace through a human so we all could find comfort, peace and forgiveness in Jesus Christ.

## Negatively Advertising God is Sin

Sir Isaac Newton's third law of physics states that every action has an equal and opposite reaction. While it's true of inertia and propulsion, I don't believe the same principle applies to our lives because when you're dealing with other human beings, every action tends to have an equal or *greater* reaction. For example, if we yell and curse, someone yells and curses back just as loud, if not louder. When we push, someone usually pushes back harder. When we mock, someone is there to mock along with us. Conversely, a smile usually begets an even bigger smile from another. A hug is repaid with a tighter hug. A genuine act of kindness encourages other kindhearted acts.

Similarly, when we engage in the practice of negatively advertising God, our words and actions can have an adverse ripple effect. Other Christians and persons may be unintentionally encouraged to react equally, if not greater, to our sin as they become involved in the same negative offenses as we are.

It's the classic mob or lemming mentality applied to spiritually. Consider the worshipper who vehemently opposes church policy or building expansion plans. Because of his criticism and outspoken protestations, he unintentionally creates warring divisions within the congregation. Or what about the Christian who misinterprets or conveniently bends Scriptures to suit her needs and agenda? She knowingly misrepresents Biblical truths, and others who aren't as Biblically versed as they should be go along with her way of thinking. Or what about the stingy Christian colleague who callously refuses to help a needy family at Christmas because he thinks they are just taking advantage of the system? His actions and opinions could influence others who might have offered up some extra money not to give as well.

In an era where the prevailing attitude is live and let live, many people harbor no shame or remorse over their sinful actions and negative advertising seems to happen with greater and greater regularity among society, including those who follow Christ. For example, years ago it was considered shameful to have a baby out of wedlock. Today, single women are artificially inseminated because they selfishly want the baby, but not the husband that should come with it. These single Moms are championed by society for their courage and "go it alone" attitude. Then there are the persons who commit salacious or sensational crimes and are turned into overnight celebrities by the media. Lying and cheating are common and seemingly accepted practices among students on high school and university campuses. Some may see it as a sign of more contemporary times, but this isn't God's way. It is the world's way. If you engage in or endorse such sinful acts and profess to be a Christian, you are simply not in harmony with God's teachings. Your stance and actions negatively advertise God by fostering misconceptions and falsities about what it means to be a true Christian believer.

There are lots of gray areas in life, but I don't think you don't need a litmus test to determine whether or not you are negatively advertising God. Simply put, when you say or do something that contradicts the teachings of Christ, consistently engage in sinful action in full view of others, blame God for your misfortunes, display lewd conduct, set a bad example, tell lies or use profanity, and refuse to accept personal responsibility for your actions, you are guilty of negative advertising. And don't think that's a complete list. These are only but a few of the ways Christians give God a bad name or hamper the work God calls them to do.

## Negatively Advertising God Destroys Your Christian Credibility

Let me share with you a trio of real life examples of how negatively advertising God can quickly destroy your credibility and undermine your attempts to spread the message of Christ.

The first incident happened one night when my neighbor invited several men in the subdivision over to his backyard to gather around a small bonfire. As glowing embers danced about in the flames, we launched into a series of mundane guy-oriented conversations. Topics centered on everything from politics to big screen HDTVs, sports to video games. A neighbor I'll call Tim soon arrived, apologizing for his lateness and announced he and his wife had just returned from their weekly Bible study. Tim talked enthusiastically about how great it was to be part of that Bible study group and how exciting it was to discover something new about God's word each week. Although three guys around the fire went to the same church as Tim, I was still proud of Tim for expressing his beliefs before the rest of us. It was one of those small things Christians need to do more often—share your passion about God and your commitment to reading and studying the Bible in front of others whether they're fellow Christians or not. You can imagine my complete surprise when, just moments later, Tim rather nonchalantly dropped the "F" bomb when sharing another non-church related story with the group.

Talk about bewilderment on my part. Minutes earlier, Tim was praising God and hyping the benefits of his Bible study, now he was using a crude four-letter word. For me, it was a total disconnect and Tim instantly lost Christian credibility in my eyes. The one word he let slip out overshadowed the dozens of great adjectives he used to talk up his love for God and the Bible study he was involved in. I couldn't help but wonder if a non-Christian was there that night (and maybe one was for all I know). Would they have had the same reaction to Tim's "F" word as I did? Would it have turned them off from the Christian lifestyle? Or worse, would they have gotten the very wrong impression that dropping vulgarity was somehow alright even after you were saved? I think Tim's actions only reinforced a common misperception about Christians that exists among skeptical non-believers and those out to denigrate our theology—most Christians are hypocrites who don't practice what they preach.

The second example of negative advertising occurred while I was channel surfing the TV. I landed on a station where the local media was covering a gay pride rally. The camera panned across a crowd holding signs of support, and then cut away to an obviously angry man gripping a large handwritten banner that read, "God hates fags." This man had it all wrong. God doesn't hate homosexuals, he hates their sin. While his obscene statement was completely contradictory to the loving nature and teachings of Jesus Christ, it could have given many anti-Christians who might have been watching the mistaken inference that the church and Christian community as a whole agreed with the man's position and hated homosexuals as much as he did. Nothing could be further from the truth. Although the vast majority of Christians follow the letter of Scripture and hate the sin of homosexuality, we are taught by God to love and reach out to homosexuals just as Jesus Christ would have. The same could be said if the sign had read God hates murderers, rapists, terrorists, thieves, liars or adulterers. God hates no one. It's sin He abhors. The misinformed man holding that sign negatively advertised God by positioning Him as a hater of people rather than a hater of sin.

The third incident of negatively advertising God happened just after a deadly tsunami struck India and Southeast Asia in December 2004. That disaster claimed well over 270,000 lives and destroyed millions of homes, villages and businesses. The massive death toll and graphic images of destruction seen on TV and on the Internet were heartbreaking. Few can understand tragedy and destruction of this magnitude, and in their anguish, many search for answers where none can be found. How could this happen, they ask? Why were so many killed? Why weren't more children spared? What could have prevented this? So many questions, never any real answers to placate us. Some find peace by accepting the callous indifference of nature. Some accept geologic and scientific explanations. Yet other voices, including reporters, relief workers, insurance adjusters and government officials angered and confused by the event, rose up and negatively advertised our Heavenly Father by referring to the wanton death and destruction as an "act of God." The same kinds of things were said after Hurricane Katrina ravaged New Orleans and coastal Mississippi in 2005.

This kind of language is bothersome to me because it implies that the God I know, love and worship is a God who intentionally causes widespread catastrophe, inconsolable grief and unbearable suffering. And when highly emotional victims and loved ones of those swept up in disaster hear others say things like that, they could come to the conclusion that if God caused this disaster, then why couldn't He stop it.

When bad things happen inexplicably, some people have a tendency to get angry with God, especially when it's the violent or unexpected death of a loved one, damage to their home and possessions after a fire or storm, the loss of a job, divorce, or any other terrible thing that happens in life. Instead of seeking refuge in God's love and comfort, they misdirect their heartbreak and blame Him for their sadness and misfortune. Because they have no healthy outlet by which to control their emotions and anguish, they let anger and resentment fester until it eventually spills out in words and actions that cast disparagement on God.

Beyond the science, it's difficult to explain why earthquakes, tornados, floods and other acts where nature wreaks random havoc occur. Why does a tornado strike down this house instead of that one? Why does a hurricane veer towards that location and not this one? Why does a forest fire turn this way instead of that way? Why does lightning strike that person and not another?

While God created the heavens, the earth and all who inhabit it, I believe some events are simply set in motion by the nuances and happenstance of nature and people just happen to get in the way. As the brilliant architect of nature, I also believe God can and will intercede if it is His will. He can absolutely direct a tornado away from your house, cause rain to dampen a raging fire, or nudge a hurricane back out to sea. What I don't believe is that He is the kind of God who takes pleasure in calamity and callous destruction of life and property. In the case of the Asian tsunami and Hurricane Katrina, who's to say God didn't intervene and save even more people from death and injury and prevent more property from being destroyed? I like to think our fervent prayers helped prevent the tsunami and Katrina catastrophes from being much worse.

Avoid giving God a bad name in times of tragedy by not using the phrase "act of God" to describe natural disasters or include such wording in your business contracts. Instead, positively advertise God and emphasize His love by praying for the victims or traveling to the affected areas and volunteer to help with food and shelter, counseling and rebuilding. Be the light that beams God's loving presence and infinite goodness for all to see even in their darkest hour. By advertising God in a positive way amid tragedy, we stem the flow of negativity and show others the goodness and grace of Jesus Christ working through us.

## Are You Negatively Advertising God?

So what about you? Do you negatively advertise God? Do you find yourself doing some things that don't exactly put your faith practices and beliefs in the best light? And if so, when? Maybe you're not one who curses and swears, steals and cheats, or attributes bad things to God, but we all are guilty of advertising God in some way, shape or form because sin is so prevalent is our lives. Here's just a few common ways in which Christians negatively advertise, shame, put down, disrespect and deny the God we love, worship and pledge our lives to.

You negatively advertise God when you...

- Live a life contrary to Biblical teachings.

- Fail to put your faith into action.

- Spread gossip.

- Judge others.

- Take pride in unethical business dealings.

- Denounce or abandon God when illness or tragedy strikes.

- Attribute false statements to or defame God.

- Trust money more than you trust God.

- Exclude people because of social class or race.

- Position God's love as preferential instead of all-inclusive.


## Be a Positive Force for God

Sin makes you say and do all sorts of foolish things that negatively advertise God. In reality, the unfortunate things you sometimes say and do that are born out of anger, frustration, indifference, or just to fit in with the prevailing sentiment of the group are very likely in stark contrast to the core Christian values you hold so dear.

I'm sure you feel badly afterwards, but negatively advertising God isn't something that's always so easy to dismiss with an apology, retraction or clarification. As favorable an impact as a positive statement for God can bring, a negative slight can leave an indelible impression about God and the church on someone as well, only in all the wrong ways. Maybe your words give someone the wrong idea of who God is and what He is all about. Or your actions and false justifications foster false beliefs as to what's accepted as right and wrong within the church.

People either see or won't see the love of Christ within you. As His representative, you have the responsibility to positively promote God and all His glorious benefits, not just in the comfortable confines of the church or your home, but everywhere you go. That means watching carefully what you say, whom you hang out with, and what you do. After all, you never really know who has their eyes and ears on you, wanting to see how, as a Christian, you'll react to a certain situation. Will you impress them as one who positively promotes God with passion and authority or be someone who offers up a bad connotation of what it means to be a Christian? Have you ever wondered how many unbelievers or those waffling between choosing or not choosing God have simply opted out because of seeing or hearing Christians act in discord with their beliefs? It may be more than you think.

Don't let the travails of daily life prevent you from staying true to the teachings of Christ and emphasizing all the joys and blessings He's given you and your family. It's a whole lot easier to be the one who's badmouthing God when the chips are down, when facing a medical challenge, or when the future seems tenuous. Anyone can do that. But you can't turn God off and on as the situation warrants. You can't be committed to Christ only in good times then grow angry and rebel against Him when times aren't going so well. It's the staunch Christian believer who stands strong in the face of adversity and positively praises God in both good times and bad that gets people's attention. That kind of unwavering love and faith on your part is what imparts in others a fervent desire to seek God's comfort and peace in their life, too.

## UP FOR DISCUSSION.

1.  List some of the ways you personally negatively advertise God. What changes can you make?

2.  What are some ways you can transform bad habits into positives for advertising God?

3.  What do others think when they see or hear Christians negatively advertising God?

4.  Do you find the phrase "act of God" personally offensive? Why or why not?

5.  How can Christians help others who've experienced a tragedy move away from being angry with God to reconciling with Him instead?

# 11

## *101 Simple Ways to Advertise God*

"Always give yourselves fully to the work of the Lord, because you know that your labor in the Lord is not in vain."

—*{ 1 Corinthians 15:58 }*

If you've read this far, you should have a very good idea of what advertising God is all about and how you can actively participate in it with more courage and confidence. Still, many people are looking for specific and practical ways in which they can advertise God every day. The following is my short list of 101 suggestions. But I know there's way more! If you have additional ideas that would help others maximize their potential for advertising God, I would love to hear them. Please e-mail your thoughts directly to me at rick@advertisinggod.com for possible inclusion on my website advertisinggod.com. Come to think of it, by sharing your suggestions, you're advertising God already!

1. Passionately proclaim your faith to all who will listen.

2. Wear a cross or religious-themed jewelry to work and school.

3. Invite someone to church.

4. Say a blessing before every meal, even when eating out.

5. Share your spiritual values with a friend or coworker.

6. Read your Bible on a park bench, commuter train or airplane.

7. Lead a prayer.

8. Listen to Christian CDs or radio stations while friends are in the car.

9. Perform random acts of kindness in the name of Jesus Christ.

10. Become a religious mentor to a confirmation teen or adult new in the faith.

11. Teach Sunday school or Vacation Bible School.

12. Volunteer for a church mission project locally or abroad.

13. Lead a Bible study group.

14. Be there for someone in need.

15. Show Christ-like compassion for AIDS patients.

16. Tell your employer you will not work on Sundays and why.

17. Add a favorite Scripture verse to your e-mail signature.

18. Keep a Bible verse page-a-day calendar on your desk or wall.

19. Invite a new neighbor or coworker to a Sunday school social.

20. Add a favorite Bible verse to your business card.

21. Share your testimony with your Sunday school class or worship congregation.

22. Follow the golden rule.

23. Live every day as if Christ were coming at any moment.

24. Give your time and money generously.

25. If you see a need, address it. Don't assume someone else will.

26. Read and study the Bible so you can share Biblical truths with confidence.

27. Don't let rules and traditions hold you back from talking about God.

28. Become a pen pal with a missionary family or a foreign child who doesn't know Jesus.

29. Discover what your spiritual gifts are and use them to glorify God.

30. Teach your children to love, honor and obey Christ.

31. Start a Bible study at work or in your neighborhood.

32. Tell rec league coaches your child will not participate in practices or games on Sundays.

33. Praise God during difficult times.

34. Participate in church outreach programs like visitation, soup kitchen detail and Meals on Wheels.

35. Tape a Bible verse to your computer screen frame.

36. Welcome visitors to your Sunday school class, then mail a note saying you're glad they came and invite them back.

37. Put a bumper sticker that praises God on your car.

38. Have t-shirts made that identify your church and wear them when doing service work out in the community.

39. Tap into your creativity…write a song, skit or drama and perform it for your congregation.

40. Add a short Bible verse or affirmation at the end of your answering machine message.

41. Create and maintain a faith-based website or blog.

42. Take that leap of faith you've been praying about and share your experience with others.

43. Offer to pray for and with someone in need.

44. Make amends with those who have wronged you and forgive them in the name of Jesus.

45. Put God first in your life and teach your children to do the same.

46. Offer to drive children or disabled adults to church and worship programs.

47. Seize your talents, using them to glorify God.

48. Write a testimonial and submit it to your church newsletter or popular devotionals such as The Upper Room for publication.

49. Tithe faithfully.

50. Ask God for an opportunity to share your faith every day, and then do it confidently and without shame.

51. Wear shirts or hats embroidered with positive, God-friendly messages.

52. Be the one who starts a new and much-needed ministry in your church.

53. Begin a church or community wide prayer chain.

54. Read your Bible every day.

55. Pray for those who mock and ridicule God.

56. Don't be afraid to speak up for what you believe.

57. Let others see Christ in you through your actions, words and deeds.

58. Try to meet and associate with new Christian friends.

59. Encourage and support friends and family who answer the call of God whatever it may be.

60. Don't let negative things said about God and Jesus Christ go unchallenged.

61. Be kind to the unkind.

62. Download and burn popular Christian music on CDs and give to unsaved friends.

63. Apply stickers with God-friendly messages to envelopes of bills and letters mailed.

64. Share a Biblical story, principle or teaching whenever you can.

65. Stay true to your beliefs and convictions even when you're outnumbered.

66. Don't worry about what others think.

67. Encourage your children to pray.

68. Show love and quarter to your enemies in the name of Christ.

69. Read Easter and Christmas stories from the Bible to your family on holiday mornings.

70. Add God-themed stickers and tags to your school backpack.

71. Actively lobby city, county and state officials on all issues that affect your church, your Christian beliefs and your values.

72. Put a God-positive magnet message on your car.

73. Buy extra grocery items each week and donate them to your local community food bank.

74. Do things for God's glory not your own ego.

75. E-mail unsaved friends your church's worship service times or a calendar of church-sponsored events.

76. Put a Christ-friendly magnet on your refrigerator or car.

77. Teach your children about the real "gifts" of Easter and Christmas.

78. When asked to tell something about yourself, say you are a Christian.

79. Say "God loves you" to someone new every day.

80. Always be truthful and honest at school and work.

81. If you own a business, print a favorite Bible verse on your billing invoices, receipts and print ads.

82. Ask to say the blessing at your company picnic or holiday luncheon.

83. Place sticky notes with your favorite Bible verse on monthly bill stubs and other communications mailed out to those you don't know.

84. Display a religious-themed screensaver on your computer.

85. Vote for politicians who share your faith values.

86. During illness or before surgery, tell your doctor you've prayed for him or her and that you have faith God will heal you.

87. Volunteer to help pay a portion of a needy family's rent.

88. Find one thing you do really well and use it to serve and benefit Almighty God.

89. Count your blessings, instead of your money.

90. Become friends with an at-risk teen or child from a single parent home.

91. Get out of your comfort zone and take God's message to the sick, the poor and the downtrodden.

92. Add a front license plate tag to your vehicle that boasts a positive God message.

93. Live out Christ's command in the great commission.

94. Focus on the things of heaven, not the temporary things of this world.

95. Store owners, display a clever Biblically inspired message or Scripture on your sign's marquee.

96. Wear a t-shirt with a thought-provoking or inspirational Scripture verse.

97. Donate Bibles and church supplies to persons, groups or missions here and abroad.

98. Phone or send a card to those lifted up in worship and let them know you're praying for them.

99. Create a community ministry where you cut someone's lawn or clean their house while they're recuperating from an illness, or help rebuild after a natural disaster.

100. Add a Scripture verse in an easy-to-locate spot on your family or business website or create a link to a daily devotional site such as The Upper Room.

101. Always make God the #1 priority in your life and be outspoken in your love for and allegiance to Jesus Christ.

# 12

## *A Last Word on Advertising God*

○ ○ ○ ○ ○ ○ ○ ○ ○ ○ ○ ○ ○ ○ ○ ○ ○ ○ ○ ○ ○ ○ ○ ○ ○ ○ ○ ○ ○ ○ ○ ○ ○ ○ ○ ○

"Be strong and courageous. Do not be terrified; do not be discouraged, for the Lord your God will be with you wherever you go."

—*{ Joshua 1:9 }*

Although I say it's the "last" word on Advertising God, it's not really the "final" word since advertising God is always evolving, always happening, always needed. Ideally, no one should have the last word on this subject because advertising God is contagious and catches on with others who see and hear you bringing others to Christ while you're selflessly doing God's work. It makes them want to pick up the cross of Christ and carry it along as they do great and mighty things in His name, too. Advertising God is not a rallying cry. It is just who you are as a Christian and should be an effortless part of your daily routine as you live a life fully for Christ.

I want to reiterate something I wrote at the very beginning of this book. Advertising God is letting others know you are a dedicated, determined and loving Christian servant through your words, actions and deeds. It doesn't have to be complicated or planned out in advance. More often than not, advertising God is a simple act or something done spur-of-the-moment that can potentially impact others in ways you cannot imagine. That's because whenever God gets involved, there's no limit to the things He (and you!) can do!

My wife Lisa teaches elementary school and she once shared a story with me that I feel sums up what advertising God is all about. Lisa told me of a fellow teacher who approached her and casually mentioned that she would not be teaching the following year. When Lisa inquired as to what this teacher would do, the teacher responded she wasn't exactly sure. She just felt the presence of God leading her to do something different. What He was calling the teacher to do she didn't know, but she had decided to confidently follow her faith, answer God's call and resign from her educator position to pursue whatever opportunity God put out before her.

I think this is exactly what advertising God is all about. Casually sharing your faith and God experiences with others with humble and honest conviction. That teacher's faith story was shared as a casual and simple answer to a casual and simple question. Whenever Lisa tells that particular story, she recalls the teacher's great faith and expresses admiration for her selfless dedication to following Christ.

To leave the security of a stable job in order to set out on an unknown faith journey goes against every rational thought most of us have. After all, we've been conditioned our entire adult lives to get a good job, bring in a steady paycheck and provide for our families. With a mortgage, groceries, car payments and college funding to think about, it's just not safe or responsible to up and leave a good, steady job, right? I'm sure the teacher wrestled with these very same concerns, just as we would. In the end, however, it was the trust she put in her faith and not in the security of her job that ultimately encouraged her to follow God's call. She didn't allow the safety of her job, the potential impact on her bank account or her financial obligations to dissuade her from doing what God wanted her to do.

As the story spread throughout her school, one woman's courageous faith, though she may never know it, lives on to inspire countless others. Though she had no pretenses or expectations of how her story would impact others when she shared it with my wife, that teacher's willingness to advertise God struck Lisa and I as powerful testimony to what Christian love, stewardship and obedience is all about. May we all strive to have that kind of unwavering faith!

## "One Person with Passion is a Majority"

On the surface, it's difficult to understand why so many Christians find it hard to bring up the subject of God or try to avoid any mention of God with unbelievers altogether. God is, after all, the author of the world's greatest book. He's grander than any car we could ever buy, more forgiving than those new tires on your sports car, more satisfying than a supreme bacon double cheeseburger, more engaging than any Hollywood celebrity, and more impressive than a world-class athlete. Think about it. God is Coca-Cola, Microsoft, GE and Wal-Mart all rolled into one. He's the maker of Heaven and Earth, the creator of all living things, the forgiver of our sins, and giver of eternal life. You don't get much more awesome than that. Christians should jump at the chance to praise God's pure and perfect grace and goodness to anyone who will listen anytime we have the opportunity.

Advertising God touts the benefits of the risen Lord and eternal life, and informs others of who God is and how He conducts business. By now, you know you can't sit back and hope someone else does the job of passionately touting the living, active and very participatory God we all love and need. Yes, such actions require sacrifice, discipline, dedication and a deep-rooted love for the one true God that transcends all our earthly burdens and obstacles. But, it's up to Christian believers like you and I to passionately, cheerfully and brazenly promote God and all His great benefits in the best ways we know how. We can do this by putting our faith into action and by taking full advantage of our spiritual gifts. We do it by never, never, not ever being ashamed to promote and advertise the God we love, worship and serve.

Convincing yourself that most people have been exposed to the message of Jesus Christ in some way, shape or form is a real cop out. And besides, that rationale is simply not true. Even in the new millennium, there are still millions of Americans and persons abroad starving to hear the word of God and who have a real longing to have someone introduce them to the Lord and His message. That someone can be you!

Ralph Waldo Emerson wrote, "Don't waste life in doubts and fears; spend yourself on the work before you." Inspirational words in Emerson's day and now sound advice for today's Christians who struggle to share their faith or put their spiritual gifts to work for God. When you play on God's team, there are no second-stringers. Everyone is talented enough to be in the starting line-up, and you should always be ready to get in on the action. Much like the coach yelling your name, when God comes calling, you should leap at the chance, drop everything you're doing, grab your gear and go all out for Him. Instead of sitting around wallowing in doubts and fears that prevent you from doing something positive, sprint out from the darkness of excuses and complacency and be seen living and witnessing in the light of Jesus Christ. Now more than ever, our Christian actions need to be seen and our voices heard.

Advertising God is one of the things that give you your Christian identity. It means you'll eagerly and enthusiastically talk up all the good things of God and Jesus Christ without being guarded, hesitant or fearful of what others might say or think. It means you have to be loud and proud because you are among the ones called by God to make a real difference in the world. It means you'll talk as excitedly and passionately about God as you will your favorite deli, that amazing shower cleaning product or the air conditioning guy you love so much. One of my boss's favorite expressions is "one person with passion is a majority." I'm not sure who said it, but I believe those seven little words hold so much truth and power. The Christian community can influence so many others to follow Christ's lead just by us collectively stepping forward, saying or doing our thing, and adapting a ready, willing and able attitude towards serving and obeying Christ anytime, anywhere, anyplace and under any circumstances, good or bad.

My prayerful wish for each and everyone of you is that after reading this book, praising and advertising God will become as easy and effortless as recommending a good restaurant, a must-see movie, a great product, or a place of business when you're at work, at school, at church, at social parties, wherever. The family of God grows one word, one action, one believer at a time. Like I mentioned earlier, living your life as a true and faithful servant is the very least you can do for the God who has given you so much, yet really asks so little of you in return.

Some days you won't feel like advertising God. Some days it will seem too tough. Some days you'll hesitate a few minutes too long and miss your chance to share your spiritual gift, your story, your passion or your favorite Scripture. It's all too easy to be the one who sits down and stays silent instead of the one who stands up for Christ and proudly declares, "Here I am, Lord." The next time God gives you an opportunity to serve, share your beliefs or put your faith into action, go for it! Because if you don't advertise God, who will?

# Notes

## CHAPTER ONE

1. The Official Mahatma Gandhi eArchive & Reference Library. 20 June 2006. <http://www.mahatma.org.in/quotes/quotes.jsp?link=qt>

## CHAPTER TWO

2. U.S. Census Bureau World Population Clock. 12 June 2006. <http://www.census.gov>
3. How Many Countries in the World? 12 June 2006. <http://worldatlas.com/nations.htm>
4. History of the Gideon Bible. 17 March 2005. <http://ky.essortment.com/gideonbible_rcwz.htm>
5. The Gideons International FAQs. 21 July 2005. <http://www.gideons.org>
6. History of the Gideon Bible. 17 March 2005. <http://ky.essortment.com/gideonbible_rcwz.htm>

## CHAPTER FOUR

7. Steve McClellan, "Fox Breaks Prime-Time Pricing Record," Adweek, 12 September 2005 <http://www.adweek.com/aw/search/article_display.jsp?vnu_content_id=1001096022>
8. Superbowl Ad Rates. 13 June 2006. <http://advertising.about.com/b/a/232373.htm>

## CHAPTER SIX

9. Cherise Williams, "On a Hot Wing and a Prayer," Atlanta Journal Constitution. <http://www.ajc.com/search/content/services/internship/story/CheriseWilliams.html>

## CHAPTER EIGHT

10. "Glorify His Name!: Commentary on the Song of Songs by St. Bernard of Clairvaux, Sermon 23, 30 May 2006. <http://glorifyhisname.com/sys-tmpl/sos23b/>

11. Michael J. Vlach, "Americans and the Bible: Bible Ownership, Study and Knowledge in the United States." 15 June 2006.
<http://www.theologicalstudies.citymax.com/page/page/1572910.htm>

12. "Five Out of Seven Core Religious Behaviors Have Increased in the Past Decade According to Barna Survey." 15 June 2006. <http://www.barna.org/FlexPage.aspx?Page=BarnaUpdate&BarnaUpdateID=232>

13. [Office of Readings, April 4…(Lib. 3, 8-10: PL 83, 679-682]. 30 May 2006.
<http://members.aol.com/johnprh/reading.html>

14. Transcript of Tony Blair's Speech to U.S. Congress, 17 July 2003.
<http://www.cnn.com/2003/US/07/17/blair.transcript/>

15. The Holy Eucharist in the Life of Bl. Teresa of Calcutta, 14 September 2004.
<http://www.catholicculture.org/docs/doc_view.cfm?recnum=6606>

## CHAPTER NINE

16. The Mind of Mahatma Gandhi, (H, 21-7-1940, p. 211). 28 April 2006.
<http://www.mkgandhi.org/momgandhi/chap04.htm>

*Advertising God* can be easily adapted into a productive, interactive series of Sunday school lessons or weeknight classes. To order your leader's guide or to purchase additional copies of this book for your group study, visit www.advertisinggod.com or e-mail rick@advertisinggod.com. To schedule Rick Sizemore, the author and creator of *Advertising God*, for a seminar, to speak with your church congregation and/or men's and women's ministry groups, or to appear at a worship retreat, please e-mail rick@advertisinggod.com.

978-0-595-40694-4
0-595-40694-7

Printed in the United States
63282LVS00005B/154-192